# there's something about Jonathan

# there's something about Jonathan

### Jonathan Richman and the Modern Lovers

## Tim Mitchell

**Peter Owen**
London and Chester Springs

PETER OWEN PUBLISHERS
73 Kenway Road, London SW5 0RE

Peter Owen books are distributed in the USA by Dufour Editions Inc.,
Chester Springs, PA 19425-0007

First published in Great Britain 1999
© Tim Mitchell 1999

ISBN 0 7206 1076 1

A catalogue record for this book is available from the British Library

Printed in Great Britain by Redwood Books, Trowbridge, Wiltshire

*For Olga*

# ACKNOWLEDGEMENTS

THERE are two people in particular without whom this book would have been impossible. My foremost thanks should go to Ernie Brooks and Tony Jonaitis, who both gave up inordinate amounts of their time to help me, and to David Robinson, in particular for help with the photographs. Much gratitude, too, to Jeremy Reed for being instrumental in getting the project this far.

Unless credited in the text all the interview material here is my own, and I must acknowledge my debt to everybody I spoke to, each of whom was supportive and did so much to contribute to the book: Roye Anderson, David Berson, Asa Brebner, John Cale, John Doukas, John Felice, Kim Fowley, Danny Fields, Michael Guardibascio, Jerry Harrison, Richard Hell, Matthew Kaufman, Lenny Kaye, Greg 'Curly' Keranen, Tommy Larkins, Gerard Malanga, Eugene Manzi, Ellie Marshall, Glen Matlock, Sterling Morrison, Andy Paley, Leroy Radcliffe, Lou Reed, Pete Shelley, Marty Thau, Brennan Totten, Geoff Travis, Moe Tucker and Alan Tyler.

My thanks, too, go to my wife Claire, to Holly, Tom, Ellie and Jake and to Bill Allerton, Joe Foster, Geoff Griffin, Goran Kraft, Les Gripkey, Jeff Barrett, Michael Heatley, Martha Morrison, Beth Groubert, Tony Barber, Clinton Heylin, Rob Stickells, Marko Stamenković, Mark Steele, Gordon Irlam, all the subscribers to the Jonathan Richman e-mail discussion list – and everyone at Peter Owen.

# AUTHOR'S NOTE

I wrote to Jonathan early on in my research for this book and asked whether it was something with which he might want to be involved. He very politely declined but said that he appreciated the interest. This is not, then, an 'authorized' account, but it is the first ever full-length consideration of Jonathan's career – and also of the original Modern Lovers – and I have tried hard to ensure that it is as accurate and complete as possible, within the parameters set by the documentation available and the inevitable limitations of people's memories.

I should point out, too, that many of the observations on Jonathan's live performances come from my own experience of his shows and that this accounts for what may seem to be the undue British, indeed London, bias. That most of the rest of the discussion of his live work concentrates on gigs within the USA is, I think, excusable, as these constitute the bulk of his live work; there is nothing intentional in the relative lack of coverage of Jonathan's many warmly received concerts in other parts of the world; it is merely a reflection of the information at my disposal.

Two other points need mentioning: from Chapter 5 onwards I have referred to the Jonathan/David/Ernie/Jerry line-up as 'the original Modern Lovers' in order to avoid confusion with the later incarnations of the same name; and I must own up to the fact that the translations of Jonathan's Spanish lyrics into English are my own.

My principal hope for the book is that it engenders a wider appreciation of Jonathan and his work – and that the reader can tell that it comes from the heart.

# LIST OF ILLUSTRATIONS
between pages 120 and 121

# CONTENTS

# INTRODUCTION

A<small>T</small> first, Jonathan Richman thought of becoming a painter – it seemed to be the way he would be able to express himself best. But then he saw the Velvet Underground play and he loved their ability to conjure up magic while people watched and listened, and he wanted to do it himself.

Jonathan began his career as a solo act but before long decided that he would benefit from the power of a band behind him. The other Modern Lovers that he gathered together soon became what Jonathan had wanted them to be more than anything – a band whose raw but acute mixture of emotional intensity, musical intelligence and crusading forthrightness made them artistic heirs to the Velvet Underground. Where the Velvets, however, had seen their pioneering work receive little financial reward, the Modern Lovers soon found themselves in a position to turn it into real commercial success.

Tragically, right from the start, the Modern Lovers contained the seeds of their own destruction. Jonathan had wanted to create a vehicle for the better and wider communication of his feelings and views. Once he had achieved this, and once the process had become a proper two-way communication, his loneliness became blunted and he began to replace his analysis of the negative with affirmations of the positive. By mid-1973, with a Warner Brothers contract, the Modern Lovers were on the verge of making it big – but their success was rooted in a past that Jonathan had transcended. With new messages to communicate he needed new Modern Lovers, and at this point the band disintegrated.

The new band that he recruited may have had different aims, but its members were going to need at least as much crusading zeal as their predecessors. Jonathan's new-found optimism was not necessarily going to be greeted with universal enthusiasm by his established audience. After much rehearsal the new band eventually toured Europe – and Jonathan found his new approach triumphantly vindicated, with packed concert halls, a single, 'Egyptian Reggae', that was a hit all over Europe and, in Britain, three successive chart successes.

By now Jonathan had rid himself of his 'negative' past and it was time once again to look to the future. This band's job, too, was done. By 1979 a second Modern Lovers had been disbanded, and Jonathan was back in Boston. He would not release another album for five years.

Jonathan had rejected fame twice, but the second time round it had been closely allied with what he considered also to be *success* and he had enjoyed it – for a while. Now he had real self-determination, now he could do whatever he wanted, whenever he wanted.

Twenty years later, Jonathan is still doing what he wants, when he wants. Over the course of the last few years Neil Young asked him whether he wanted to join his record label, Vapor – and he did – and the Farrelly brothers asked him whether he wanted to score and appear in their hugely successful film *There's Something About Mary*, and he wanted to do that, too. Conan O'Brien, the American chat show host, often asks him whether he wants to appear on his nationally networked TV show, and that's another thing he likes.

What he likes to do best, though, is to sing in front of his own audience. Then Jonathan gives performances that are unique, with an intimacy that has no parallel. He will relive the emotion of his songs and create new dimensions for them (improvising both lyrics and instrumental passages), relate anecdotes that illustrate their inspiration, dance, laugh and charm his way into the hearts of the crowd. Along the way he will play some of the most accomplished and expressive guitar you could hope to hear.

This is what he always wanted to do.

# 1 I GREW UP IN THE SUBURBS

Natick, Massachusetts, in the far western reaches of Boston, impaled on Route 9. A halfway house between the city and the open highway . . . a blandness between the bleakness of subways, expressways and skyscrapers and the magic of neon, radio towers and 'fifty thousand watts of power' . . .

JONATHAN Richman was born here on 16 May 1951. His mother was a remedial reading teacher, his father a travelling salesman. The landscape and environment within which he would grow up would profoundly influence his thoughts and movements and therefore his early songs which, right from the start, would always express his feelings and actions as honestly as possible.

Jonathan's parents were conventional; Jonathan, from an early age, was anything but. His next-door neighbour for eight years, before becoming a founder member of Jonathan's first band of Modern Lovers, was John Felice. For him, their part of Boston was 'just a dead boring suburb. It was tract-housing, flat, just single-storey ranch houses – really ugly and nothing exciting going on.' Jonathan's parents may have felt at home here, but their son did not. As he grew, he would soon feel the need to explore the poles of his world – that city and highway – and to escape its middle ground.

Jonathan was the first of two boys. His musical influences started early; in adult life he was to recall being sung to as a two- or three-year-old by his parents; his memory was of having been very moved by music from this time on. By the age of five he was spending his days drawing pictures – and chasing girls. Their failure to reciprocate his affection made him confused and hurt. His friends were few and

**15**

Jonathan felt far apart from the people around him and their social relationships. The loneliness that was to inspire and inform his early songs was already large in his life.

Between the ages of three and seven Jonathan dreamed a lot. His dreams he later described as elusive, both in their content and in their failure to translate themselves from the unconscious to the conscious, to reality, experience and memory. Dreams would continue to be important to Jonathan into his adolescence and adulthood, when he would claim to be able to access and influence them and to achieve the translation for them that he had earlier desired, where dream-state and reality would no longer be mutually exclusive.

Despite his loneliness, an upbringing that he would later describe in an interview with Kristine McKenna as 'bland' but not 'bad' was taking shape around him. Jonathan's parents were honest, hard-working and respectable. They were keen for their eldest son to be a success, and he wanted that as well. For him, though, that meant succeeding in voicing his feelings and in a public advocacy of sincerity and passion. In the staid kind of society to which his parents belonged the achievement of these aspirations would be more likely to be looked on as failure. To his parents' credit, however, they took their disappointment in their eldest son's aims in their stride and were later supportive of Jonathan's early career. While they plainly had problems understanding him, their love for him was never in doubt. He himself, although making it clear that his attitudes are very different from theirs, has never criticized the way he was brought up.

If Jonathan was misunderstood and isolated at home, he was many times more so at school, which was disciplinarian and illiberal, and he longed to escape. Rebellion, however, was a more realistic short-term solution to the problem, although in his case it did not take any of the conventional forms. Instead he broke rules that no one had even realized existed. On one occasion, bored, he drew two circles with indentations on his trousers and was summoned to the principal's office. Asked to account for his action, he replied that he had drawn the bass and treble dials of an electric guitar. It was 1962, Jonathan had discovered rock and roll and he reckons that it may just have saved his life. From this time on, throughout his childhood and adolescence, a transistor radio was to be his permanent companion.

The previous year Jonathan had made his first awestruck visit with his parents to New York. Having been inspired, too, by rock music, twin wonders of the modern world had been revealed to him and he could see a whole new landscape, far away from the restrictions of his upbringing, opening out in front of him. His ambition was to leave school as soon as possible and to explore this new world. His parents, however, were keen for him to continue with his education in order to acquire some insurance for the future. They were to get their way, as Jonathan did eventually make it to graduation day – his dreams of leaving were not to be fulfilled just yet. (Towards the end of school, his parents would actually have to pay him to stay on, and he would later put his survival there purely down to the salvation that rock and roll offered him.)

Jonathan's first-hand musical experiences began in 1965 with what was to be a three-year relationship with the clarinet; this gave way to the more rock-and-roll-friendly saxophone for a couple of years. By 1966, Jonathan had also started playing the guitar, an acoustic which his father, despite his misgivings, had bought for him. (His father was also later to buy him his first electric guitar and his first amplifier.)

During this period, rock and roll's development was gathering pace and Jonathan, despite his love of the music that had filled his childhood, was alive to the new possibilities. In early 1967 he heard a song on the radio that was like nothing he had heard before and he was intrigued enough to make a mental note of the band's name: the Velvet Underground. Shortly afterwards a friend acquired a copy of the album from which the track had been taken, *The Velvet Underground and Nico*, but didn't like it and, looking to get rid of it, played it for Jonathan. Jonathan had already earmarked a Fugs record from his own record collection as a possible trade. His friend put side two of the Velvet Underground album on the turntable, and the first bar of 'Heroin', with its icy guitars, was enough to give Jonathan the kind of chill that comes from an awareness of great beauty. As the record played, side by side with this there came a recognition that this was music that would speak personally to him. He saw in the Velvet Underground's songs, and the way they presented them, a sincerity and honesty, a power and a beauty that were to inspire him.

Shortly after this Jonathan began making the first of several appearances in print for local Boston magazines, *Vibrations* and *Fusion*. *Vibrations* was much like the fanzines that sprung up in the punk explosion of the late seventies; put together on a shoestring budget, it survived from one issue to the next. Jonathan would contribute drawings as well as stories and reviews. *Fusion* appeared more regularly, had its own offices and a larger budget and later went on to publish its own books. It was well regarded for its espousal of new poets, and Lou Reed, in particular, found a welcome outlet for his poetry in its pages. In the March 1967 edition of *Vibrations*, a review of *The Velvet Underground and Nico* by Jonathan was his first attempt at bringing their music to a wider audience – something he felt he had a duty to do. In September's issue he wrote a piece on the 'erotic power' of the Velvet Underground and the New York art scene.

It was the same year, 1967, that the sixteen-year-old Jonathan first began performing in public. By long tradition the Common at Cambridge, Massachusetts, was made available for musical performances on Sunday afternoons; Jonathan, knowing one of the organizers, decided to make use of the opportunity and loaded up his father's station-wagon with his small amplifier and guitar. He played his early songs on bills with bluesy, boozy acts like the J. Geils Band, to what was generally a mixture of bemusement and derision. As John Felice recalls: 'What struck me most was that he just looked so naked there. Jonathan had really short hair and dressed completely different from anyone else at the time. This was back in the hippy days when everyone was stoned out of their minds on acid and shit. Some of the people would yell: "Get off the stage, man!"'

Jonathan's trademark was a white vinyl Harley Davidson jacket, and he played a turquoise Fender Stratocaster slung low down by his knees. Sometimes this guitar would only have two strings on it, and sometimes it would have the full complement – but he might use only two anyway. His facial expressions were various and intense. Although his technique was minimal and his singing voice unconventional, the emotion behind his songs and their performance was enough to create a positive reaction in at least some of his audience – three or four admirers out of each group of a hundred or so would be enough to keep him going – and among these were David Robinson, who was to become the drummer for the Modern Lovers, and Danny Fields, later to be instrumental in bringing them to public attention.

Although the Cambridge Common was the main outlet for Jonathan's music at this time – he became a regular there, asked back after each performance – he would also play on street corners for anyone who was prepared to listen. Despite having been very lonely throughout his childhood and, as John Felice, who was one of his few friends at the time remembers, sometimes 'brooding, moody and dark', he had never been shy. From an early age he had always had supreme confidence in himself and in the way he saw the world. It was therefore no problem to him to play his songs in environments that were at best indifferent and at worst hostile. He wanted to sing them so badly, to communicate at any cost, that nothing else mattered.

To communicate better with his audience, Jonathan had to learn to play better, and he would constantly practise his guitar alone in his room, loud enough to be heard all over the neighbourhood. For Jonathan, as a solitary teenager, the electric guitar was a powerful extension of himself, literally a way of amplifying his feelings. Not only were they amplified they were also reciprocated, with their beauty enhanced via the harmonics and resonance of an instrument that was itself beautiful. Perfectly proportioned, it was smooth to the touch and also infinitely responsive to it.

With his dreams, his guitar and his songs, Jonathan had alchemized his ideal girl, a perfect companion in his loneliness.

Sometimes Jonathan's father would take him along in the car as he travelled around New England selling food to army bases. Other people might have regarded the landscapes through which they drove as either unworthy of comment or even as a succession of eye-sores, but Jonathan's eyes widened at the sights that spread out in front of him: advertising hoardings, road signs, the 'stop'n'shops' and Howard Johnson's restaurants and motor lodges, the fried chicken and Coca-Cola stands. Their brightness and colours, their promises that guaranteed fulfilment – none of these was going to turn away from him or let him down – were magical to Jonathan.

These stations of light and colour, connected by neon highways, were what inspired his early songs: 'Ride Down on the Highway', 'Howard Johnson's' ('I see the restaurant/It is my friend'), 'I Grew Up in the Suburbs', 'Roadrunner'. Their lyrics contrast Jonathan's extreme loneliness with the excitement he felt at his discovery of another world, a new environment that would stimulate his imagination rather than stifle it. The Howard Johnson's not only appeared in his songs as subject matter, they were physically there as well. After an initial period playing an Epiphone guitar, Jonathan had bought a Stratocaster. Cutting a piece out of it, he spray-painted it a unique shade of 'Howard Johnson' green, and then replaced it – embedding in the instrument of his feelings their very real inspiration. Jonathan was trying to come to terms with his own solitude and to create power and beauty there. Whenever he saw this adaptation reflected in his environment he embraced it, as witnessed by John Felice. 'We used to get in the car and we would just drive up and down Route 128 and the turnpike. We'd come up over a hill and he'd see the radio towers, the beacons flashing, and he would get almost teary-eyed . . . He'd see all this beauty in things where other people just wouldn't see it. We'd drive by an electric plant, a big power plant with all kinds of electric wires and generators, and he'd get all choked up. He'd almost start crying. He found a lot of beauty in those things, and that was something he taught me. There was a real stark beauty to them and he put it into words in his songs.'

'Roadrunner' is an exploration, a celebratory but lonely journey through the Boston night, a post-Velvet Underground 'Sister Ray' for a new, potentially more positive age. It is an emotional travelogue through the colours and lights flashing out of the darkness of Route

128, summed up in the improvised line from the version that was to appear on the 'Beserkley Chartbusters' album: 'I feel alone, I feel alive, I feel a love.' The song draws on Jonathan's experiences while out with his father and with John Felice, travelling around Massachusetts; it adds to them what he saw and felt cycling as a child around Natick and then intertwines them within the structure of a composite night drive. It takes its format from the Velvet Underground's 'Sister Ray', abbreviating the three chords of its riff to just two and adopting its semi-improvised narrative and musical arrangement. (These are both songs that could never be played the same way twice.) The highway in 'Roadrunner' makes up for the absence of a lover – it takes her place. Its speed and lights flood the senses – substitutes for love and sex. The car radio is a constant, providing a sound-track to an escape from boredom and pallor into excitement and colour. Music and release inspire each other. The propulsion of the two-chord rhythm is the perfect framework for a classic driving song. In the version on *The Modern Lovers*, organ slashes and snarls burst out of it like cars flashing by in the night and buildings looming out of the darkness. On a cold, dark, moonlit night the beat of the car on the road is like a heartbeat, and the band – one massive rhythm section – recreate it. When, outside the city, the car hits open road, the organ solo cruises along with it – bass chords removed, echoing the empty spaces where nothing is visible for miles around. Then the car slows, and a cry of 'Roadrunner once, Roadrunner twice' brakes the narrative drive before both pick up speed again, accelerating through the gears, the band shouting repeatedly: 'Radio on'. Speed blurs, with the insistence of the tempo, and settles on high as speedometer and VU needles peak. The frenetic, hypnotic pace continues relentlessly until the drive nears conclusion – and then the momentum decreases, decelerating chords killing the pace. Both car and song cut back and ease down until, finally, both are brought to a halt.

By summer 1967, the Velvet Underground were playing regularly in Boston, which had become a second home to them, a place where their music could be heard away from the Warhol/Factory scene which seemed inextricably linked to them whenever they played in New York. Their usual venue was the Boston Tea Party which was part-owned by Steve Sesnick, their manager. Jonathan felt sure that the members of the band would understand him and soon introduced himself, as Moe Tucker, the band's drummer, remembers. 'He would come to the shows and come very quietly into the dressing-room, which was huge, and just stand and watch and listen. It took him a few visits before he spoke to anyone, but when he did we all liked him immediately. He was obviously very intelligent and well read and was fun and interesting to talk to.'

The late guitarist Sterling Morrison had similar memories. 'The first time I saw him that I remember was as an alert little kid at the Boston Tea Party in the afternoon, while we were there setting up and fooling around. I just remember his smiling face, and then we saw him every time after that. He went to all the Boston shows, and he was around us before and after . . . Jonathan would always play you his latest song, whenever you saw him – if he had a guitar he would show you what he had just come up with . . . If the Velvet Underground had a protégé, it would be Jonathan.'

John Cale, the Velvets' multi-instrumentalist, recalls: 'The Boston Tea Party itself was kind of a wreck. Jonathan would show up persistently with poems, scribbled poems, that he had written about this, that and the other, mainly about the band. We had no idea initially he was going to be a musician.'

At first glance there seems to be little logical reason for any link between Jonathan and the Velvet Underground. Jonathan was fired from the beginning by a strong moral determination which was often to provide the subject matter for his songs and would always inform them, whereas Lou Reed was keen to profess his own moral detachment in the writing of his lyrics. This apparent contradiction is reconciled, however, by the honesty that underpins the work of both writers. Reed was able, by detaching himself from the people he was writing about, to see their behaviour objectively. Jonathan, by the absolute candour of his self-expression, often to the cost of risking ridicule, has always been able to inspire in his listeners the certainty that what they are hearing is the truth. Jonathan and Reed both acknowledge and need the possibility of redemption by love, which can transform despair into hope.

The Velvet Underground provided Jonathan with what was his first large-scale public performance, when he opened for them and the Grateful Dead in Springfield, Massachusetts. Jonathan talked about this show a lot both before and after it happened and it was hugely important to him. It put him on the same stage as his heroes, in a sense equating him with them. Nervous beforehand, but with excitement outweighing fear, he successfully completed a short set, as Sterling Morrison recounted. 'Jonathan asked if he could open for us, and we said: "Can't see anybody stopping you!", and he said: "Can I use your guitar?" and I said yes. He used my old Gibson 335 and a Vox Super Beatle. I guess he played four, five or six songs, "Howard Johnson's" among them, to an . . . uncertain effect on the audience.'

By 1969, after occasional visits to New York to see Lou Reed and the Velvets, during which time he also met Andy Warhol at the Factory, Jonathan had graduated and, his obligations to his parents fulfilled, was determined to pursue a career as a performer. Now he was finally free to escape. He decided to make New York his new home.

The relocation itself was perhaps no big deal for an eighteen-year-old with his confidence, but to try to build a career there alone, and pretty much from scratch, was a substantial undertaking. Jonathan knew something about city life, but New York, in comparison with Boston, was much more extreme: vastly larger, more culturally diverse and with a sharper divide between rich and poor. Although theoretically providing more opportunities, competition was also that much more intense, and making an impact would be that much more difficult. Jonathan knew something about playing in front of an audience – but not a New York audience.

Once he had arrived he renewed the Velvet Underground connection and found himself a place to stay for a couple of weeks on Steve Sesnick's couch in his East 55th Street apartment. At the end of the fortnight Jonathan moved into the Hotel Albert which, despite its Fifth Avenue address, was the far from glamorous, rat-infested home of many musicians. Here he would practise in the basement with his electric guitar. He would later remember being flattered by the impression he gave (largely down to the volume of his playing) to a member of the Blues Magoos who, when walking by one night, thought that he was in fact a whole band.

During his stay in New York Jonathan furthered his friendship with Danny Fields, begun at the Cambridge Common shows. Danny, shuttling between New York and Harvard, where he had attended university in the early sixties and still had friends such as Susan Blond and the late Ed Hood, had met up with Jonathan at these shows and, as a fellow admirer of the Velvet Underground, found they had much in common.

Jonathan had also got to know Andy Warhol's right-hand man, Gerard Malanga. 'I don't remember exactly how I met Jonathan, it may have been through Danny Fields or a friend of mine named Tony Pink, but I think my first recollections are of him needing a place to stay. That was back in 1970, and he would crash at my flat from time to time.'

Jonathan kept in constant touch with John Felice over this period, and they would write back and forth as much as twice a week. Jonathan would detail the books he was reading, the music he was listening to and the goings-on at Max's Kansas City, the rock-and-roll venue that was a regular haunt for the Velvet Underground/Warhol crowd. Jonathan was also at this time indulging the love of food that would continue to be one of his great pleasures and would give John accounts of his favourite restaurants: macrobiotic, vegetarian and Middle Eastern.

Jonathan had a series of short-lived jobs in New York, including messenger for Esquire magazine, busboy at Max's Kansas City and rack-puller in the garment district, but found attempting to launch his musical career frustrating. So much so, in fact, that on one occasion he took to the roof of the Hotel Albert with an unamplified electric guitar and shouted his songs to the pedestrians eight floors below on University Place at 10th Street. When the police arrived Jonathan disappeared.

By the summer of 1970 Lou Reed, tired and dispirited, had effectively wound up the Velvet Underground – although different incarnations of the band would continue to use the name for another two years – and Jonathan, a solo career in New York seemingly as far away from fruition as when he had arrived, decided that it was time to return to Boston. New York had been electric, nervy, unpredictable, overwhelming and hilarious – all at the same time – and the overall effect had become grotesque. It was time to forsake an environment that had never really suited more than a part of him.

Before returning, however, Jonathan decided to make a brief foray to Europe – later to be recalled in the song 'Nineteen in Naples' on the album *I'm So Confused* – from where he went on to Israel to stay with his cousin. Here, at Masada, he immediately fell in love with the desert. The miles of sand were a perfect contrast to New York; it gave him a breathing space and the aridity was a fertile ground for his imagination.

Refreshed, he made the journey back to Boston, determined now to form a band – the actual decision had been made while staring at a full moon one night in Jerusalem. He wanted an environment where he could perform regularly and establish a base. Also, as he would later explain, he was lonely and he wanted friends.

Back home Jonathan met up again with John Felice. John was a guitarist and had been keen to form a band with his friend and neighbour for quite a while. Now was finally the right time and Jonathan had his first band member.

Looking next for a drummer, Jonathan walked into a record shop in Kenmore Square and started writing out a three-by-five-inch card to put on the notice board. As he got to the word 'drummer' a voice came from behind the counter saying that if he ever wanted a drummer, he, David Robinson, was the man for the job. David had seen Jonathan play on two or three occasions on the Cambridge Common and had been sufficiently impressed, despite the sometimes hostile reception accorded him, to commit himself to joining his band. David had already been playing for some time and, living in a house full of musicians, was looking for a musical project to which he could commit himself.

It was indirectly through David Robinson that the Modern Lovers acquired their next recruit: their first bass player, Rolfe Anderson. Rolfe was attending the Art Institute of Boston at this time. One lunchtime a co-student invited him down to the record shop in Kenmore Square to meet David. Introductions made, David told Rolfe about the band Jonathan was assembling. (Rolfe and David are not, as has been written elsewhere, cousins.) A few nights later Rolfe went over to David's house and auditioned. He took to the songs right away and, although feeling that he was not necessarily on the same wavelength as their writer, recognized that here was a project worth pursuing. The others liked his bass-playing and the band was complete.

They needed a name and Jonathan, after much deliberation – it had to be something that summed up both his message and the way it was to be presented – settled on 'The Modern Lovers, the Danceband of the Highways' ('the Danceband of the Highways' was very quickly dropped). As he recalled in a 1978 Dutch radio interview, he had initially written down about twenty possible names, including Jonathan Richman's Rockin' Roadmasters, the Rock and Roll Masters, the Rock and Roll Dance Band, the Modern Dance Band, the Suburban Dance Band, the Suburban Romantics and the New York Romantics.

The band rehearsed two or three nights a week in David's basement. Rolfe would come over from school and hitchhike back. The material was mainly Jonathan's early songs like 'Roadrunner', '(When You Get Out of the) Hospital' and 'She Cracked', interspersed with a couple of cover versions of songs by the Kinks. Rolfe remembers Jonathan issuing instructions to the other band members such as 'Keep it simple' and 'Turn the volume down' and waving his arms downwards for emphasis – nothing should be allowed to interfere with the songs themselves and their messages. Jonathan's own rhythm-guitar-playing was unashamedly basic – true to the legacy of the Velvet Underground. The songs were learned one by one; Jonathan would start playing and the others would join in, playing pretty much what they wanted initially but with Jonathan editing as the arrangement developed, until the song sounded as he wanted.

The band made its live début in September 1970 at Simmons College, Boston, supporting the Sidewinders, a band who were soon to become associates and rivals of the Modern Lovers. The Sidewinders' lead singer was Andy Paley, who had first met Jonathan through his appearances on the Cambridge Common and whose career has been linked with Jonathan's ever since in a variety of ways. He recalls the start of their friendship. 'We had a lot of friends in common, but we were really rivals early on. We always had mutual respect, but when one guy's the lead singer of one band and one guy's the lead singer of another band -- plus we did gigs all the time together – you're not always good friends. It wasn't like enemies or anything, we just paired off later and started becoming very, very good friends.'

Simmons College was to become a regular venue for the Modern Lovers, as it already was for the Sidewinders and other local bands such as Aerosmith. These three bands played many gigs together, alternating as headliners. Aerosmith had yet to achieve the phenomenal popularity of their later years, and success, such as it was at this time, was pretty much shared between them all.

The Sidewinders were to go on to record an album for RCA, produced by Lenny Kaye, later of the Patti Smith Group, who was then spending a lot of time in Boston and was a keen observer of events there. Smith herself was also a fan of theirs, often recording their gigs, and Andy was later to repay the compliment by playing keyboards for her on a European tour. Even Jonathan was later to figure briefly, and intriguingly, in the history of her band.

The Modern Lovers soon began to perform live regularly at a variety of venues, including Simmons College, the Cambridge Common, youth centres and churches. Public reaction was much the same mixture of bemusement and derision as had previously greeted Jonathan's solo performances. One gig in particular, at Cambridge YMCA in Central Square (a small venue with a comparatively large stage), where a section of the audience spat and threw cans from the balcony, was recalled by Rolfe Anderson during an interview in *Trouser Press* in 1979. Jonathan seemed to thrive on the conflict produced on occasions like this but would never actually provoke it. The intention was to present an honest statement, simply, directly and powerfully. A mixture of love and hostility, incomprehension and joy was to continue to characterize audience responses to the Modern Lovers and is one that Jonathan still encounters to this day.

In early 1971 Danny Fields was talking to one of his old Harvard friends, Susan Blond. Susan had been in a couple of Andy Warhol's films and was a painter at the Museum School in Boston. She said she had two musician friends that Danny might like to meet and introduced him to Ernie Brooks and Jerry Harrison, who were students at Harvard University. Danny decided that Jonathan should meet them and arranged to bring him round to the flat in Cambridge that Ernie and Jerry shared. When he arrived he was wearing his white plastic motorcycle jacket and started dancing to the record that was being played – the Velvet Underground's last album, *Loaded*.

Jonathan talked about his love of the Boston highways, about the life bursting up out of the open roads and the suburban landscapes, and Jerry and Ernie felt that this was a vision they could share. Jerry was studying film at the time as a part of his Harvard course and Jonathan's ideas tied in with a project of his own that he was planning. As a result he filmed and recorded Jonathan, David and Rolfe playing 'Ride Down on the Highway' and also shot footage of Jonathan talking to camera as he walked around a local supermarket. The resulting material was incorporated into a larger piece which was course work for his degree. Ernie and Jerry attended several performances of this initial version of the Modern Lovers and felt that this was something with which they would like to get involved.

In the spring of 1971 they agreed to become part of the Modern

Lovers, and Rolfe Anderson, whose lack of complete unanimity with Jonathan even early on had now reached its inevitable conclusion, left. Rolfe says he still has good memories of his time as a Modern Lover, though. He keeps in touch with David and bumps into Jonathan 'once in a blue moon'. He went on to play in the highly rated Human Sexual Response.

Back in 1971 the Modern Lovers prepared to make their move.

# 2 I'M STRAIGHT

ALTHOUGH in terms of material the Modern Lovers' new formation continued where the original unit had left off, with the new members learning the songs that were already being performed, the overall sound was inevitably changed by the addition of Jerry's keyboards.

The extra instrumentation meant that when they played live there was more room to accommodate the options available: Jonathan singing only, with the musical backing left to the rest of the band, Jonathan playing guitar throughout, Jonathan using the guitar for instrumental asides and solos or abruptly cutting short his playing, as if, as Rolfe Anderson puts it, creating a piece of punctuation within the performance of the song. Jerry's keyboard sound could be eerie and mysterious, sharp and aggressive, or mournful and beautiful, to suit the songs as they now began to develop in relation to the new possibilities. Unusually for a keyboard player, distortion was a key element in Jerry's sound. At this time he was playing a Farfisa Mini Compact organ and a Fender Rhodes electric piano. These (the organ less frequently) were passed through a distortion unit made in Boston by a company called E.U. Wurlitzer which produced what Jerry considered 'the most obnoxious sound from a fuzz pedal' (for example, the effect produced for the solos on 'She Cracked' from *The*

*Modern Lovers*). While other bands were looking for soft distortion, the Modern Lovers were after the hardest and nastiest they could find (Jonathan loved solid state distortion and had a particularly raw-sounding amplifier). As well as using a traditional guitar player's tool, the fuzz pedal, Jerry took his technique from guitarists more than from keyboard players, favouring a solid, thick sound over the arpeggios that were customary at the time.

The foundation of the songs, Jonathan's original chord patterns or Jerry's recreation of them, would stay much the same but, with a larger band presenting them, they now had a fuller sound, giving them greater impact. There was strength, too, for the band, in numbers. Everyone brought their own ideas, and on stage they became a more physical presence, more of a force to be reckoned with in their proclamation of what was often an unpopular message.

Although their live set stayed much the same, some of the songs that the earlier line-up of the band had been playing did not last long.

'Cosmic Jet Plane of the Arcane' deals with jealousy and 'stealing' a girl from someone else, justified (in an echo of 'I'm Straight', Jonathan's ultimate statement of self-conviction) by a feeling of superiority, of deserving her more. Moral certitude here verges on the undignified and perhaps it is not surprising that the song did not stand the test of time. Jonathan would return to the subject many years later in 'My Career as a Homewrecker', on the album *Having a Party With Jonathan Richman*, and do it real justice – the years in between bringing a detachment that leaves room for a certain amount of self-criticism.

'She's Taking the Pill or Me' is a wish-fulfilled mixture of pride, gratitude, celebration and a certain amount of selfishness, as an intense, self-absorbed relationship between two people together against the world expresses itself in sex. She takes the contraceptive pill for him, and he is proud, grateful, glad – and certain that she is right to do it. Again, on reflection, Jonathan probably saw a lack of dignity that led him to stop performing the song. In an interview with Nick Kent years later he would say that the band had never played it again after his twentieth birthday.

'I Remember the Time' is a lament for the lost innocence of a girlfriend who has 'wasted herself with creeps'. She is a 'desecrated schoolgirl', and there is more than a hint of unrealizable dreams, together with an element of contempt that Jonathan would later dislike and disown.

A tape of one of the new band's early live performances (venue unknown and with Jerry's keyboards barely audible) features a version of 'Someone I Care About' that comes with a frenzied guitar solo from Jonathan, drenched in distortion, a 'Modern World' that urges the girl to whom it is addressed to 'Do all the things that hurt/And our love will work' and, in 'I'm Straight', an onslaught full of outspoken bravado, with verses unfamiliar from any recorded version.

As some of Jonathan's earliest songs vanished from the band's repertoire, showing that his writing was already progressing, in a similar early movement towards renewal even the songs that made up the current live set, such as 'I'm Straight', would soon start to take new shape – the verses mentioned above would disappear from performances within weeks.

The band, in their new form, continued to play the same sort of venues, but, with Ernie's and Jerry's Harvard connections, they were now able to play college 'mixers' for student audiences. The phenomenon of the mixer is described in the band's song of the same name, a.k.a. 'Men and Women Together', which is critical of the 'cattle market' atmosphere of these events, demeaning to both sexes. It makes its point with a clarion call of opening chords followed by pumping bass and, in the instrumental break, percussive rhythm guitar. Lyrically succinct, it is a classic example of one of the Modern Lovers' concise 'message' songs.

For the band, mixers were more often than not unsuccessful attempts to present their music to an audience that was embedded in a youth culture of commercialized blues-rock and R&B, with its more 'adventurous' members tapping into the quasi-classical bombast of Emerson, Lake and Palmer and Yes. To be faced with a band who revelled in the rawness both of the emotions in their songs and of the technique with which they played them was to come up against a bucketload of reality – and that was not what these audiences wanted from their groups. The Modern Lovers were conceited enough to believe that they were something special, and receptions like this did nothing to convince them that they needed to be more modest; in fact, as a result, they were merely confirmed in their belief that what they were doing was important. At a time when 'musicianship' was everything, and songs were becoming longer and more self-indulgent, the logical progression of a culture steeped in too much dope and acid, the Modern Lovers were following a completely different line, one that had been gouged out against the grain of contemporary rock music by the Velvet Underground and the Stooges. The Modern Lovers played songs that were short, very sharp and often pointed straight at some of the things that their audiences held most dear. Shaking up the music business is something that is supposed not to have happened until 1976/7, when its whole constipated structure seemed, for a short while, to be under threat. In 1971, though, paralysis was already setting in – one band could see it and was determined to strike at its heart. This is how Jerry Harrison sees the band's attitude to music's prevailing spirit: 'We were like the original punk band. Most music had gone away from heartfelt things towards professionalism. We put inspiration first.'

The Modern Lovers glorified true love, sincerity, passion, faith and the power of the soul to survive everything the world could throw at it. They pilloried insensitivity, insincerity, self-indulgence and materialism. Jonathan's songs were a mixture of anguished cries for affection, attacks on hippydom, drugs and artifice and espousals of old world values in modern world settings. The band were always going to have to struggle to get this message across, but the rejection and opposition that they encountered only made them stronger. Jonathan continued to thrive in an atmosphere of hostility, but this did not arouse bitterness in him. It even enabled him to say on one occasion, as Ernie Brooks recalls: 'Well, we know you don't like us, but we love you anyway.' Jonathan would engage the contradictory elements of an audience and turn their aggression back on themselves, with the intention always of making them think and question. In John Felice's eyes, 'He was an original confrontational punk, way before anybody else was doing that kind of thing. A lot of the angst of his teenage years was really upfront in the early days; it was black and white, right in the face. He wasn't afraid to say how he felt, and if it hurt people, or if it stepped on their toes, so be it.'

Sometimes, if an audience was not paying enough attention, Jonathan would stop the band and say: 'This is important, so I'm going to recite the lyrics.' The audience would be startled enough by the abrupt curtailment of the song that Jonathan would immediately have the attention that he wanted. Sometimes, too, songs would be prefaced by spoken verses – to similar effect, lyrics in rock and roll rarely being highlighted in this way.

(When the band was in California in 1973, recording tracks for what should have been their first album, they played a notorious gig at the Swing Auditorium in San Bernardino, supporting Tower of Power at what had been planned as a showpiece gig for Warner Brothers. Rubbish was thrown at them by a predominantly redneck crowd who took great exception to both their music and their lyrics. David Berson, assistant to Warner Brothers president Mo Ostin and the man who was eventually to sign the band, remembers this reception: 'The audience was incredibly hostile; there were all kinds of screams of "Go back to Boston where you belong!" It seemed to me that they were quite happy to keep on playing in the middle of the storm. The songs were totally unique; no one else was singing anthems to being straight and songs advising kids not to die now because "Someday we'll be dignified and old".')

Lack of comprehension and often outright hostility from their audiences was something the Modern Lovers shared with the Velvet Underground and the Stooges who had had similar experiences. A sense of solidarity with their favourite bands was further confirmation of their conviction that what they were doing was both important and right.

While Ernie and Jerry, when they first joined the Modern Lovers, were sharing a flat in Cambridge with two other students, David was living with his parents in Woburn, just north of Boston, and the band were able to use the family basement as a rehearsal room. Soon, however, they decided to look for a house in which they could all live and rehearse together and found one in Cohasset, south-east of Boston, where they proceeded to set up their equipment in the living-room. Here their lifestyle was fairly minimal, relying as they did on food parcels from Jonathan's parents and living very much from one day to the next. Sometimes, too, Jonathan's mother would bring him clothes – once it was a large woollen sweater that she, to his embarrassment and immediate refusal, insisted he put on straight away. Despite their lack of funds the months that the band spent here and later in a second house in Cohasset were to be something of a golden age for them.

Although Jonathan was able to continue to get the band the type of gigs they had already been playing, it was left to Ernie and Jerry to arrange dates in the city – but even here there was little money to be made. Sometimes a hall would be booked, the mayor's permission would be obtained, police would be hired and, with eighty-odd people turning up, there would be nothing at all left for the band. They also played at teen centres out in the suburbs and at small clubs, such as Stonehenge in Ipswich, with a similar lack of remuneration. None of these places paid more than two hundred dollars a night, and expenses such as petrol and the rent of a van would usually account for most of that.

Apart from the more conventional halls and clubs, the band would also venture into territory that was relatively unexplored in a rock-and-roll context. Sometimes they would beg the owners of coffee houses more used to folk acts and poetry readings than rock music for the chance to play and, on a one-night-stand basis only, a new venue would be created. More unlikely still they also played at hospitals and old people's homes. For these performances the band would have to play very quietly, which suited Jonathan fine – even at this stage of his career he was going through phases where he wanted volume reduced to a bare minimum. At the old people's homes, John Felice says, Jonathan would 'ham it up big time, and they would love him! He would play right into them, and they'd eat it up like you wouldn't believe. He charmed the pants right off them. He would put

on this Charles Aznavour act, and we would be in the background,
barely playing.'

In the same vein, the Modern Lovers also played for children in
hospital. In contrast with some of the 'proper' gigs, where the reaction was often hostile, the children, like the old people, really
appreciated anyone who made an effort to come into their environment and cheer them up. These shows were some of the most
satisfying the band played and ones to which they began to look forward. They didn't really change their set much on these occasions,
although some of the more bitter songs, such as 'She Cracked', would
be excluded.

The band would drive themselves and their equipment to gigs,
sometimes in Jonathan's father's station-wagon and sometimes in
their own catering truck. But the rest of the band would only travel
like this on one condition – that Jonathan didn't drive. He was a *bad*
driver but not, as David Robinson points out, *reckless*. He drove as
though he had just been given his licence: nervous, unable to take
turns smoothly, to relax and go with the flow.

Since working in New York and returning to Boston Jonathan had
spent little time in conventional employment, but he had, somewhat
remarkably, driven a cab for a while – until losing a passenger out
of the door one day. The hours of a self-employed cab driver were
appropriate to his lifestyle, but the fundamental problem was that
Jonathan was never going to be suited to anything that resembled a
regular job; financial income, even if small and irregular, was going
to have to come from his music.

The members of the band, living and working together, were subject to the usual pressures this brings: Jonathan was naturally untidy,
David was organized and ordered, Jerry and Ernie were somewhere
in between, and a certain amount of conflict was unavoidable. They
had a common purpose, though, and a mutual loyalty and friendship
that bound them together. The band would often go out together in
the evenings, but Jonathan also liked to walk around the city on his
own. At other times he would stay in his room and read while the
others went into town. Jonathan had the knack of being able to fall

asleep at any time, anywhere, sometimes snoring loudly, oblivious to what was going on around him. On waking, refreshed, he was known on occasion to sit up and immediately start writing lyrics for a new song. His powers of concentration were such that even if there were ten people in the room at the time distraction was not a problem.

Despite the fact that a little of Jonathan's acute loneliness was dissipating – he had friends and he lived with people who shared some of his ideas and attitudes and helped him to express them musically – it would continue to underpin most of his writing over the next couple of years. Real love – romantic, reciprocated love – was still missing from his life, and so his songs had to carry on demanding and pleading for it. The early material, like 'Roadrunner' and 'Howard Johnson's', had isolated him in a series of impersonal environments as he lived out his loneliness, alternately strengthened by its confirmation of his self-determination and weakened by its denial to him of warmth and companionship, and although some of his newer lyrics would start to range wider in the way they dealt with this isolation it would be obvious in every line that it was still at their core. 'Cambridge Clown' is about Jonathan's alienation from the young men of Cambridge and his failure to reach into the hearts of its girls. Around him he sees potential being wasted, while at the same time he feels his own power flowing through him, and the contradiction brings him tears of frustration and bitterness. 'Such Loneliness' has deceptively jaunty, electric piano-led verses describing the overpowering effect that New York had on Jonathan, his rejection of the self-destructive lifestyles of some of the girls he met there and a link between his current loneliness and that of his childhood. The chorus slows the pace right down and relentlessly hammers home the message of the title: that Jonathan's isolation is almost too much to bear. 'Girlfriend' is one of the most melodic of Jonathan's early pieces and expresses, alongside its loneliness, a yearning that is fulfilled in a dreamlike way, as he imagines life with a girl with whom he is at one. Easy-paced, the song is carried by a stately piano combining, towards its end, with electric guitar in a majestic instrumental passage, as the union between Jonathan and his girlfriend is conjured up.

Before they shared a house together Jonathan would often ring up Ernie in the middle of the night and tell him about the dreams he had had. On one such occasion Jonathan, convinced that he had actually entered, on the astral plane, into the dream of a girl he really cared about, was worried that he might have disturbed her waking mind. He was so convinced, and convincing, that he managed to persuade Ernie that it had really happened. This form of travel through the unconscious was, for Jonathan, an alternative reality and, more than that, it was an intermeshing of two minds and spirits, producing the deepest possible intimacy between two people.

The opening of 'Astral Plane', with Jonathan alone in his room, sets the scene for a psychic journey that conjures up the magical means whereby an unreciprocated love can be reciprocated by projecting it sideways into another world – that of the astral plane – and backward into one that has already passed – a previous life. A love that may, as far as the girl is concerned, be non-existent is made not only real but eternal. Jonathan is in the extremity of isolation, but there is still a mystical, time-written reason to believe that his love must be mirrored by the girl's. The astral plane is the place where the impossible can become real, the place where dreams come true, where Jonathan can tell her everything that he cannot in real life and where she will understand and respond in harmony with him. The song's eerie Doors-like organ and hypnotic bass give it a dreamlike resonance and propulsion, the vocals are anguished but insistent – Jonathan believes absolutely in what he is singing and wants his listeners to believe.

Dreams were a refuge for Jonathan, but, more than that, they were also a way of bypassing time, providing a link with the eternal. They were an alternative reality, every bit as real as daytime life. Some of the best drawings he executed at this time were inspired by his dreams and he would also return to the subject in later songs such as 'Here We Are in Dreamland', 'New England Summer Song' and 'Wake Up Sleepyheads'. In the course of the latter, a classic verse–chorus–middle-eight punk rush with Velvets-inspired rhythm guitar, he dismisses his girlfriend's adherence to Freud – dreams are not there to be interpreted, they are real – and urges the youth of Boston to 'wake up' to the possibilities of sleep.

'Hospital' was written at much the same time as 'Astral Plane', about Jonathan's experiences in New York at 'places like the Samuel Ruben Dormitory', as he would later remark during a live performance. Again, the song concerns the absent object of Jonathan's affections, but this time he knows where she is and why she is there. Sometimes when the Modern Lovers played this song live Jonathan would have a drawing on stage on an easel, a street-scene, and he would point to it and say: 'These are the streets, this is the house where she lived.' Seven years later, on stage in New York, he would still remember her apartment number. 'Hospital', like 'Astral Plane', tries to avoid the pain of the present by looking back to the girl's past but also forward to her future – with him. There is the same sense that by the sheer force of his willpower his love for her will be returned. The 'power in her eyes' shows that she can be redeemed by his love, despite the things about her that scare and sicken him. The song's melody is starkly beautiful, expressing yearning for a love that he cannot bring himself to believe is doomed. Sometimes, reliving the emotion of the events he was describing, Jonathan would cry during performances of 'Hospital'.

Tears would also come to him on stage at other times, but no one would ever claim that they were anything other than absolutely genuine, as David Berson emphasizes. 'He cried on stage more than any other performer I've ever seen. He'd pick up the microphone stand, he'd be pounding it into the stage and crying, and girls in the audience would be throwing him their handkerchiefs. They'd be saying: "Oh, Jonathan, don't cry!" The great thing about Jonathan was that he pulled all this stuff off with an air of just the most naïve and benign sincerity. It wasn't as if he would smirk because he had evoked the response he was looking for; he would be grateful for the handkerchiefs! The tears would pour down, and he would wipe his eyes ... Jonathan was incredibly sexy, he had these incredibly sexy moves, and then his tears just made these women want to hug him and take him home.' John Cale also comments on the emotion of his public performances and their impact on the female members of his audience. 'He was always charismatic. He had a lot of magic, especially when he got carried away – you never knew what was going to come out next. It was like a patois of housewives' tales.'

The strength of mind that lies underneath the loneliness of songs like 'Astral Plane' and 'Hospital' bursts out into the open in 'I'm Straight', a song that demands attention, grabs it and will not let go. 'I'm Straight' was the number with which the Modern Lovers used to begin their sets, and it was like a manifesto, ensuring that their audiences got the message right from the start. It is hard to imagine today the effect it had then. A large proportion of the typical audience would already be well on the way towards drug-induced stupor by the time the band appeared on stage; they would be self-assured and secure in the environment of a rock-and-roll gig, with people around them whose behaviour and attitudes mirrored theirs: anti-parents, anti-authority, pro-hippy, pro-drugs. Suddenly a band appeared in front of them who used the form of rock music, the music of rebellion, and a noisy, raw version of it, to preach opposition to their sacred cows, to rebel against them. This must have been massively disorientating and threatening, and it is hardly surprising that sometimes their reaction was one of verbal and sometimes physical hostility. 'I'm Straight' shouts out loud that a drug-addled mind is a mind that is repressed, one that has given up sensitivity, freedom of thought and imagination, one that deserves no respect. The band's pride in their values and message was never as strong as when they delivered this song. Originally the object of Jonathan's disgust in the song was called 'Hippy Ernie'; a few months after Ernie Brooks joined the band as a courtesy to him this was changed to 'Hippy Johnny'. It had never actually bothered Ernie, as it happens, but the thought was there – Jonathan made it clear that he would never sing anything that other members of the band might find offensive.

Jonathan's approach to song-writing and song construction was fairly straightforward. He would usually have a set of lyrics (although the band were given the opportunity to edit these and suggest new directions for them) and a melody, and the basic structure would remain intact. Around this base, though, there would be room for the band to add musical surroundings and, at certain points, instrumental sections. Occasionally Jonathan would present a song that was unfinished and the band would complete it.

Jonathan, then as now, was a prolific songwriter, and pretty much anything of note around him would be used as material; John Felice remembers that he even wrote songs about television commercials. As a result, a lot of songs would be presented at rehearsal, played a couple of times and then dropped. Jonathan was his own harshest critic and more often than not he would himself jettison what was substandard. In an interview for *Andy Warhol's Interview* magazine in 1973 he would say that the melodies of his songs derived from the words and that any lyric that did not have an intrinsic melody would be thrown away. The melodies, too, had to be suited to his voice – and to the general vocal possibilities of anyone else who wanted to sing them.

On stage, although some songs were more or less set-pieces and would vary little, others could take on new aspects both musically and lyrically. They could develop through the band's improvisation or Jonathan's ad-libbing of monologues, changing of lines and addition of new verses or, as already noted, they could be prefaced by Jonathan's spoken introductions. Some of these consisted of a verse or two of the song's lyrics or slight variations on them, others were specific to the occasion.

Visually the Modern Lovers were unpretentious with a marked lack of excess at a time when ostentatious behaviour was particularly fashionable. What really made them stand out, though, was Jonathan's appearance. He not only rejected the uniform that was then regarded as an expression of rock-and-roll outrageousness, he went to the opposite extreme, wearing stiff-collared, clean white shirts, plain white T-shirts, trousers that were straight rather than flared (often grey slacks), sneakers rather than platform soles, occasionally pointed shoes. For him fashion might have had its own place, but that place certainly was not on a rock-and-roll stage – that was purely for presenting songs. He rejected the appearance and manners of the rock star, as well as the attitudes, right from the start. He never put pressure on the rest of the band in the area of dress, however, and David, in particular, provided quite a contrast, always *au fait* with style innovations such as the use of nail varnish and keen to employ them himself. (Even at this early stage there were latent warning signs of some of the differences in areas such as this and Jonathan's attitude to volume that would much later contribute towards forcing the band apart.) With his short, neat hair (he would go to the barber's and get a 'business' cut) and 'straight' style of dress, Jonathan looked as though his presence at the heart of a rock-and-roll band was an aberration. Although this was certainly not an act (that would have been a distortion of his true feelings and would therefore have been allowed no place in his performances), he was fully aware that it would set him apart from other bands and create a reaction in an audience – and that was certainly part of the attraction.

Stage clothes were interchangeable with everyday clothes for Jonathan, and he was intent on appearing smart and clean-cut wherever possible. In the same 1973 *Interview* piece he described this attitude to his appearance as a rejection of artifice in favour of honesty: sneakers do not exaggerate the wearer's height, short hair exposes the face, T-shirts reveal the arms and 'my arms tell you a lot about the kind of work I do'. Intriguingly, Jonathan also mentioned methods of dress later espoused by punk progenitor Richard Hell: the wearing of torn clothes and spray-painted white T-shirts. And, tellingly, he was unconvinced of his own proposals, worried about being misunderstood and thought disrespectful.

Modern Lovers gigs were often publicized by the band themselves, using posters and handbills featuring their own artwork. David constructed many of these, using simple graphics ideas rather than drawings. He often incorporated the trademark heart with one side shaped like a fin that Jonathan had devised and that would eventually be used for the cover of *The Modern Lovers*. Jerry also contributed using the heart symbol or, more usually, Letraset, as he recalls. 'I remember one in particular I made. We were playing this kind of snooty junior college, a girls' school, so I made it in script, as though it was a formal invitation, and then I went and got some cheap lipstick and I kissed them, so they had lips on each one.' But it was Jonathan who provided most of the material, sometimes using collages and more often drawings, including figures of the band. (When he, John Felice and David Robinson were first looking for a bass player, Jonathan had put together a cartoon-like poster, prefaced by 'We Love:', it featured a humorous list of the band's preoccupations.)

In the autumn of 1971 the Modern Lovers made their first appearance in a recording studio, Intermedia in Boston. Intermedia was the first 24-track in the city and was later bought by the Cars. By this time the Modern Lovers had already attracted the attention of Warner Brothers, and it was one of the company's East Coast A&R men, Stuart Love, who arranged the recording session and who first made David Berson aware of the band. Only four songs were recorded; one of them was the version of 'Hospital' that was later to appear on *The Modern Lovers*, the others were a frantic version of 'Roadrunner', deeply rooted in 'Sister Ray', a similarly raw 'Someone I Care About' and 'Ride Down on the Highway', with which the band use to close their live sets, a prelude to the encore of 'Roadrunner' that used to follow it.

'Someone I Care About' was one of Jonathan's earliest songs, one he had been performing before the Modern Lovers existed. In its original form it was observational as well as personal, watching 'Hugo' fail in his pursuit of 'Mary', but the recorded version is a devastating rejection of power and selfishness in relationships, emphasizing instead the need for sincerity and commitment, even in the face of physical violence.

Ernie Brooks says that 'Ride Down on the Highway' was the band's signature tune, and thematically it is a distillation of eternal romance and late-night journeys along the Boston highways that is possibly the most uplifting of Jonathan's early songs – a vision of an earthly paradise.

Around now the 'Harvard Mixer' gig later to feature on the various different versions of *Live at the Long Branch Saloon* took place, and it was a vibrant performance with long spoken introductions, changes of pace (a menacing 'She Cracked'), unusual songs ('Walk Up the Street', a cover version of ? and the Mysterians' '96 Tears') and some new lyrics: in 'I'm Straight' 'Hippy Ernie' (not yet 'Hippy Johnny') has a 'Woodstock brain' and an 'acid face', he is 'spineless Ernie – hey, where's his backbone?' Alongside the lonely intensity and occasional bitterness that informed a lot of Jonathan's work, in live performance there was also plenty of opportunity for him to exercise a self-deprecatory sense of humour that would provide a strong contrast. On this occasion it showed itself when John Felice was given the chance to introduce 'Wake Up Sleepyheads' – and took it gleefully, describing the song as 'one of the worst songs that I've heard in my whole life' and 'refusing' to play on it. Reminded by Jonathan that all he really objects to are the lyrics and that he doesn't have to sing, only play, the performance finally began. The set ended with a rather sluggish 'Roadrunner' – but one studded with improvised lines.

Although Boston was their home, the band, if anything, now found their reputation growing faster in New York where Jonathan had previously become acquainted with the influential circle of which the Velvet Underground had been a part. They would also play a few low-key gigs here, at loft parties (where Lenny Kaye remembers seeing them play 'in an alcove') and, as John Felice recalls, at 'a bar in the Village'.

Apart from his stay there in 1969–70, Jonathan also made other, shorter visits to New York around this time – accompanied, on one occasion, by John Felice. Jonathan would appear at Andy Warhol's Factory on these occasions and, says John, 'hang out on the periphery'. Although far from a central figure then, he still developed friendships with several of the regulars, including Gerard Malanga, Danny Fields and Ed Hood. The Factory crowd considered Jonathan weird but in the right way, one that corresponded with the ethos there. Jonathan did not especially like the classification, but he liked many of the people, and the Velvet Underground tie-in legitimized the connection.

The New York–Cambridge shuttle eventually brought more and

more of the *cognoscenti* to Modern Lovers' gigs. People like Gerard Malanga would come along, dance and then file rave reports when they got back home, and soon a very real excitement began to grow up around the band, with comparisons being made between them and the Velvet Underground. Strange characters would turn up to these gigs and film them, and there were soon hip parties with money and drugs splashed around. Jonathan was unaware of the presence of the latter – and would have strongly disapproved had he known.

Ed Hood, ex-Warhol Superstar, lived in Boston at this time, and his apartment there was a focus for much of the town's rock-and-roll life. Ed could usually be relied upon to be around until the small hours of the morning and to know anything of importance that was going down.

Danny Fields had been involved with Andy Warhol and then the Velvet Underground before helping to bring the Doors to public attention and going on to sign the MC5, the Stooges and, later, the Ramones. Having known Jonathan since the late sixties and having introduced him to Ernie and Jerry he was not at all surprised to hear of the Modern Lovers' increasing reputation and, in the winter of 1971, headed up to Boston with a friend of his called Steve Paul to see them. Steve Paul was in the management business and already looking after people like Edgar and Johnny Winter; the Modern Lovers were just the sort of smart, sharp young band he and Danny Fields needed. After watching the gig they introduced themselves backstage. Danny was very impressed. 'They were great. There was just a buzz about them, and so we pursued them ferociously.' In the winter of 1971 he invited Lillian Roxon, rock critic of the then huge-selling *New York Daily News*, to come to see the band at the Speakeasy, a small bar in Cambridge. She wrote a rave review of their performance at the end of one of her columns and triggered an explosion of record company interest that may well, in its intensity, have been a factor in the band's eventual disintegration.

# 3 DON'T LET OUR YOUTH GO TO WASTE

ARLY 1972 saw the Modern Lovers accelerating away from their position as a Boston-based band that also had a few admirers in New York towards a place in the national, if not international scheme of things. Lillian Roxon's article had aroused the interest not only of major record labels but of management, and a large part of the months ahead was to be spent weighing up the different offers from both these sections of the music business. It is a huge irony, given this state of affairs, that the band were to be, eighteen months from this point, without either a record deal or a manager, on the verge of disintegration, their promise to a large degree unfulfilled.

Although the Modern Lovers were starting to receive offers from many different record companies, including David Geffen's newly created Asylum, the two leading contenders were A&M and Warner Brothers. Matthew Kaufman, who was later to found Beserkley Records and be heavily involved in Jonathan's early solo career, flew out to see the Modern Lovers as joint representative, with Alan Mason, of A&M. Mason had already played him a tape of 'Roadrunner' and 'Hospital' and Kaufman was impressed enough to make an early (rejected) offer to manage the band.

By early spring A&M and Warner Brothers, in a music industry first, agreed jointly to pay for the travel and hotel expenses of the

Modern Lovers as the band flew to California to see what each of the two rivals had to offer. David Berson remembers the arrangement as unusual but pragmatic, the co-operation founded in mutual benefit, as costs were split and each record company was given the chance to see the band perform live and to record with a chosen producer.

Part of the reason for this bizarre link-up was the Modern Lovers' insistence that they were different and that they wanted to be treated differently. The decision they would make would be based not purely on financial grounds but on artistic considerations as well – and they made this clear to both organizations before the trip was agreed. Artistic considerations, however, even at this early stage, were tipping the scales in the direction of Warner Brothers. They had John Cale, formerly of the Velvet Underground, and he was already an admirer of the band. 'When I was doing A&R at Warner Brothers someone kept sending me this tape. It was a small reel with "Hospital" on it that was really interesting because it was so tentative and unsure – but that became its strength in the end. I thought it was great that somebody could just be very weak and use that quality . . . I put them in a studio in Pasadena that had a pipe-organ and they did what is now the record.'

Inside a week, the band recorded two sessions – the one with Cale was at Whitney Studios and the other with Alan Mason and Robert Appere at Clover.

For Mason and Appere, they recorded three songs, two of which, 'Girlfriend' and 'Modern World', were later to appear on the album *The Modern Lovers* released by Beserkley in 1975. The third, 'Dignified and Old', would later be added to Rhino's and Rev-Ola's re-released versions.

'Modern World' kicks off with a drum roll and then launches straight into rhythm-guitar-heavy, Velvet Underground-inspired proto-punk, punctuated by stop-and-start, primal rock-and-roll gear changes. A rejection of cynicism, dry book-learning and lack of self-respect, it recognizes the beauty to be found in the modern world and attempts to weld it to a perfect love and thereby create nothing less than an emotional utopia. Isolated by his loneliness, Jonathan could stand back and identify more clearly than most exactly what he wanted; propelled by the pent-up force of his frustration, he had the power to go and take it. 'Dignified and Old', its minor key and rhythmic force creating a mixture of beauty and power, is like a response to Pete Townsend's 'My Generation', a plea to the 'kids' to stick with life and transcend sorrow, to grow, mature and acquire the dignity that will accompany what must have seemed an impossibly far-off fulfilling old age. For Jonathan rock and roll had always had the capability to encompass not only the ephemeral but also the eternal – and he wanted them both. Able, in youth, to savour the mystery and particular potency of a special moment, he also wanted the clarity and positivism that would allow him to keep that ability for the rest of his life. Not for him rock music's classic 'live fast, die young' burn-out. The message, in rock-and-roll terms, was revolutionary, but there was no reason for anyone who empathized with 'My Generation' to be alienated from it. Its starting point, bitterness, and the prospect of death in youth was, of course, exactly the same. The difference is that Jonathan lifted up his eyes and saw the finish-line, too.

These Appere/Mason tracks showed what the band could offer and were perfectly respectable in terms of their production, but it was the more substantial Cale session that really took off.

Although this album's worth of material was never originally intended for release, and was therefore regarded for years merely as a demo, Cale managed to recreate here the passion of the Modern Lovers' live shows and encase it within a discipline that produced arrangements and performances that were both tight and imaginative. Cale instructed the engineers on how to set up the microphones and treated Jonathan's vocals with reverb and high treble, reducing his natural nasality. Clarity was maintained throughout, even during the guitar/organ battles of the instrumental breaks – if Cale had produced the Velvet Underground's *White Light/White Heat* it might have sounded something like this.

The session was essentially a run-through of the band's current live set, but only about two-thirds of the material was later to make its way on to *The Modern Lovers*. Left out were versions of 'Modern

World' (harsher than Mason's and Appere's, with some alternative lyrics), 'Girlfriend', 'Love's Loneliness' and a very similar 'Roadrunner'.

'She Cracked' is an account of an initially promising relationship prised apart by the contrasting self-destruction and self-development of the two partners. It is perhaps the Modern Lovers' most ferocious recording. A relentless one-chord riff is hammered out by guitar and heavily distorted keyboards, and the pace is fierce, only letting up briefly before it charges off again towards an abrupt conclusion. 'Old World' is the companion piece to 'Modern World'. It refuses to dispense with what is old just *because* it is old and expresses another revolutionary thought, for a rock-and-roll song, in its proclamation of filial love. Bookending all this, however, is an affirmation of the vitality of the modern world and an acceptance of its inevitably greater importance. For 'Pablo Picasso' the band swap instruments, something they would also do when playing the song live. As well as being an expression of the band's rejection of virtuoso musicianship and preference for performances that came from the heart, this arrangement also brought something akin to a musical 'cubism' highly appropriate to its subject. Usually Jonathan would stay on guitar, Jerry would play drums, Ernie would play second guitar and David bass, but for this recording another change was made: David recreated Jerry's drum part and, in turn, taught him the bass part he usually used. If Jerry was playing bass, though, it must have been somebody else beating that piano to within an inch of its life – Cale, of course, whose experience of violence against that particular instrument was as long as his love for it was deep. The guitar solos here are murderous combinations of precision and aggression, the sound alternating between clean, staccato flurries and fuzz-laden blizzards, with the distortion pedal cutting in and out towards the end and then giving way to a series of tremolo howls. The song fades in at the start and out at the end, as if it lives for ever – an eternal retelling of the story of Pablo Picasso, of his irresistible passion and spirit. Cale later added a mellotron part to the version of 'Girlfriend' recorded at this session, giving it a certain grandeur, even if it does not quite have the precision of the Appere/Mason take. His viola had also been at hand in the studio, although in the event it was never used. Despite the fact that his career as a producer was still in its infancy, Cale had already produced *The Marble Index* for Nico as well as the first Stooges album – for all sorts of reasons, then, he seemed to be the ideal person to go on to produce the band's first album proper.

However, even though they were keen to work with Cale, the Modern Lovers had not necessarily decided that they wanted to work with Warner Brothers and, on returning to Boston after their brief stay in California, this was one of two big decisions to be made. The other was a resolution of their continuing deliberations over management.

While in California, the band also did some live work. One gig was at the Long Branch Saloon, Berkeley, and part of it is reproduced on the *Precise Modern Lovers Order* CD, originally released as *Live at the Long Branch Saloon*. As Ernie Brooks says in his sleeve notes this was a slightly ramshackle performance, even by the Modern Lovers' standards, but full of both charm and conviction. Jonathan addresses the audience at several points, on subjects such as the 'Jewish Princess' concept and the band's attempts to 'give you a feeling for the East Coast', and the set comprises a good cross-section of their material, from 'Womanhood' to 'I'm Straight'. There is a rare cover version here, too. In their live sets the band would occasionally perform '96 Tears' or, like the Clash a few years later, the Bobby Fuller Four's 'I Fought the Law', but by and large they concentrated on their own material. This crisp version of the Velvet Underground's 'Foggy Notion' is a collector's item, particularly as the original version was years away from release at the time and, when it did finally appear, would feature slightly different lyrics from those that Jonathan employs.

Danny Fields and Steve Paul were still, some months down the line, very interested in the Modern Lovers and, on the band's arrival back home from California, Steve Paul invited them to stay at his house in Greenwich, Connecticut. The idea behind this was that Rick Derringer, who had been producing bands managed by Steve

Paul such as the Edgar Winter Group, would produce an album for the Modern Lovers as well. Steve Paul's house doubled as a rehearsal studio – although the basement where they practised had walls lined with white tiles, giving it more the appearance of a butcher's shop – and, while out in Connecticut the band continued their live work, too. One of these appearances was as support to the Edgar Winter Band, and it was the first time that Ernie Brooks's parents had seen him play. The band were booed, and Ernie was mortified. It was with this gig that Danny Fields's attempts to sign the Modern Lovers finally came to a halt. 'That particular audience wasn't very receptive, and people got discouraged – I remember the night very well – and told Jonathan that we didn't want to work with them because we didn't think they had a future. I wasn't in a position to argue . . . Someone else in Steve Paul's organization, whom he trusted, as a musical guy, thought that the Modern Lovers had no commercial potential.'

With neither the gigs nor the management/production partner-ship working out, the Modern Lovers returned once more to Boston. As it happened, Kim Fowley, maverick producer, recording artist and provocateur, was touring here in the summer of 1972, promoting his *I'm Bad* album – and also on the look-out for local talent. While in town Fowley was approached by Maxanne Satori from WBCN, an admirer of the Modern Lovers and keen to further their cause. She persuaded him that they were worth hearing and arranged for him to listen to a demo tape. Fowley duly played the tape, which he loved, and noted a similar link between the Modern Lovers and Lou Reed as there was between the Byrds and Bob Dylan. He heard the influence, too, of bands like ? and the Mysterians in their sound. Fowley then phoned Jonathan and introduced himself. He arranged to return to Boston at the end of his tour in return for a place to sleep.

A fortnight later Fowley had it: the floor of the basement in David Robinson's parents' house. What had been agreed as a stay of a couple of days, however, was to turn into one of a couple of weeks and, according to David, his parents still talk about it.

David Berson describes Kim Fowley as 'an incredible character, a hype machine' but emphasizes that he 'sincerely loved the Modern

Lovers and Jonathan'. Although Jonathan's motivation was very different from his, he had a similar grasp and love of great pop music, as Fowley points out. 'Jonathan understood the '96 Tears' connection . . . He liked the 1910 Fruitgum Company as much as he liked Picasso, so he was fine.'

Fowley's attempts to stir up interest in the band included a recording session in the home of sound engineer Dinky Dawson. Here the band put down eight songs – all in one day, as Fowley explains. 'Dinky Dawson had a dog giving birth to puppies, and if this dog had been disturbed by us all leaving the room, we would have been attacked . . . We were all frightened of the dog!' Previously unrecorded among these songs were 'Walk Up the Street', 'Dance with Me', 'Don't Let Our Youth Go to Waste, 'Song of Remembrance for Old Girlfriends', 'A Plea for Tenderness' and 'I'm Straight'. The session was taped using the band's PA put through a 'revolutionary' system of tiny speakers, with a mix highlighting keyboards at the expense of guitar.

'Walk Up the Street' is one of Jonathan's loneliest lyrics, set to a primitive two-chord riff and here featuring piercing, treble-high guitar introduction and solo. The song starkly sets Jonathan, aged seventeen, walking through Back Bay, Boston, 'lonely and scared' at five o'clock on a Sunday morning, the temperature zero. Filled with an overflowing sense of isolation, the streets are his only refuge from complete hopelessness, but the salvation they offer is bitter and unfulfilling. There is no 'up' side to this loneliness as there is in 'Roadrunner', no euphoric insight inspired by its bleak strength and no sense of individual power. A frozen defeat and desperation are at the song's core, and they radiate out to its every point.

'Dance with Me' puts the coldness and isolation of 'Walk Up the Street' in direct contrast with a girl's warmth and the security that she offers. In its plea for his own exploratory, aware sensibility to be found a home in an affectionate, nurturing environment, the song echoes 'Girlfriend', but this is a song about the reconciling of extremes. She may be 'warm' where he is 'cold', but she is also 'dull' where he is 'excited'. The song's peak, built on sustained organ chords reminiscent of the Velvet Underground's 'Ocean', is an attempt to get her to share his love of the city. The dance of the song's title will also be their symbolic coming together, a fusion that will make whole their coldness and warmth, security and excitement.

'Don't Let Our Youth Go to Waste' is a piece of astonishing musical and lyrical bravery. Sung unaccompanied, it would usually be the final encore, as Ernie Brooks remembers. 'It was sort of a closing message. If the audience had liked us, they liked that a lot, if the audience was bored, that was something they would think was stupid and ridiculous.' Over the course of a minute and a half, this ode to a lover promises her the empathy of true love, experiences that will light up her life and forgiveness for any wrong that she does, showing a passionate concern for her happiness and a desire for her personal fulfilment. It also, starkly and sincerely, attempts to understand and to feel her physicality as a woman, to 'bleed in sympathy with [her]'. To a male-dominated society treating menstruation as either dirty, laughable or unspeakable, this stark song, starkly delivered, is a body blow delivered with clinical force. Sometimes Jonathan would cry when he sang it live. His audiences would either cheer or they would jeer – either way, they couldn't fail to react, and the message would be conveyed.

'Song of Remembrance for Old Girlfriends' is a much more relaxed affair, a gentle paean to what might have been and what never could be. Backed by electric piano and occasional washes of percussion, and punctuated by an instrumental section featuring a guitar/piano duet similar to that of 'Girlfriend', the song flows along a nostalgic path that, at its end, leads to a wish for future happiness. Jonathan would describe it during a live show as 'the closest we get to a drinking song . . . and it's not too close', which is how Ernie recalls it, too. He also sees a connection with the romanticism of Yeats, a poet they would often discuss together.

Although most of the Modern Lovers' songs were brief and to the point, there were exceptions. 'Roadrunner' of course was one, another was 'A Plea for Tenderness'. This is an epic, cathartic examination of Jonathan's ideas of modern romance and a detailed, argumentative attempt at persuasion of the validity of those ideas. Featuring a similar keyboard arrangement to 'Songs of Remembrance', Jonathan here improvises extensively, rapping about love, literature, dignity in the modern world, drugs, cigarettes, alcohol, make-up, cats, school, Lauren Bacall, television – linking relationships in general to his own in particular – before winding the song up to a finale that rejects the negativism of the girl to whom the song is addressed and attempts to replace it with an optimism about men's attitudes to relationships.

Kim Fowley took the tapes of the session back to Los Angeles with him but was unable to arouse any record company interest in them. Most labels, he says, were looking for another Grand Funk Railroad or James Taylor. There were influential figures who took an interest, however. Producer Jack Nitzsche (of Rolling Stones fame and also an early supporter of Phil Spector) was one, as Fowley recalls. 'He said: "This is the most significant rock and roll band in the world", and he said: "This record will change rock and roll." What a great quote, and Jack isn't generous with compliments.'

A gig at Ipswich's intimate Stonehenge club from this time saw Jonathan in fine form. He was loquacious and buzzing; this small venue with an enthusiastic audience was the ideal setting for him. The band were in their element, too, conjuring up a musical storm.

The opening 'Modern World' tore along, with an extended improvisation worthy of the Velvet Underground, and a long guitar/organ duel was the centrepiece of 'She Cracked', creating a fiery atmosphere to be temporarily cooled down by a rendition of 'Womanhood', for which Jonathan politely asked the audience whether they would like to dance. Short and sexy, 'Womanhood', which was never recorded in the studio, is a celebration of female power and male awe that alternates staccato chords in the verses and a sustained rush in the chorus, mirroring the beat of the first moments of sexual attraction and the dizzy swirl following it. The version of 'Roadrunner' that ended the first set has Jonathan, fiercely seizing the chance to communicate his emotional state to a receptive audience, keening between the lines – loneliness and solitary pride made public, and that clash producing, by its contradiction, a uniqueness and strength of feeling and sensation that take him over completely. The bitterness of 'Pablo Picasso' was a 'punishment' for the audience because 'we don't like the way you've been behaving', and to show the band members' 'complete contempt' they would swap instruments as well – all except for Jonathan, who would concentrate on staying in tune. The song itself was at its most primitive and hard-hitting, grinding along remorselessly and marked by twin guitars jangling, repetitious and bell-like. 'That's the sound of the New York kid beating his head against the wall.' Towards the end of the set, the band played 'I Grew Up in the Suburbs', one of the best songs they never recorded. An account of the background to Jonathan's youth, it sets Natick's 'giant screaming highways' against his loneliness to paint a picture of mental and physical bleakness.

At the end of the summer the band, in a coup of grand proportions orchestrated by Jerry and Ernie, moved to a beautiful new house in Cohasset, a mansion near a lake, with tennis courts, a gardener in regular attendance, ten bedrooms and a huge yard that led down to a private beach. The owner was working for an ambassador in Washington; Ernie remembers him as 'a very stuffy, conservative guy'. John Felice had graduated from high school in the summer and he also lived at this house after a period during which he had temporarily left the Modern Lovers to continue his education and to play in his own band. During this time away he had enjoyed the freedom of playing his self-penned material but had missed playing with Jonathan (despite the memory of constantly being told to turn down his guitar). Ernie and Jerry, for their part, had missed the sound of two guitars and were glad to see him return.

The Modern Lovers moved in on 1 June and were to have the house until 2 September. Although they had very little money, they had beautiful surroundings and a confidence in their music and attitudes that had now been recognized and confirmed by the record companies and managers fighting for their signatures.

On the management front Marty Thau, who was looking after the New York Dolls, had been asked by Warner Brothers if he would be interested in taking on the Modern Lovers as well. At the end of the summer he flew down to Boston from New York to meet them. Thau was working with the management team Leber and Krebs, who at this time were also managing Aerosmith and Ted Nugent.

The Modern Lovers had seen the New York Dolls play in Boston and liked them. The Modern Lovers considered themselves a raw rock-and-roll unit and the New York Dolls were nothing if not that, so there was a certain kindred spirit between these two punk precursors. The bands also had friends in common, like Danny Fields who had met David Johansen, lead singer of the New York Dolls, at Max's Kansas City (where, of course, Jonathan had worked as a busboy), and now began what would be a loose musical and social association.

Thau had heard about the Modern Lovers but did not know much about them. Over the course of about three days he stayed with them in Cohasset, drove around town with them, talked to them and listened to their rehearsals. In the end, he decided not to get involved, announcing his decision to Warner Brothers on his return to New York. There were two reasons for this: one was the extent to which his time was already taken up with the New York Dolls; the other was that 'I came out of it feeling that Jonathan was very far removed from your typical rock star sensibility. I didn't think he was living in the real world in some respects. He had thoughts like: "Well, if we do concerts, we'd like to have the lights on in the theatre", off-the-wall ideas about how he wanted to reach the people. Maybe there was some merit to some of his ideas, but in a sense it was a waste of time to even be thinking like that – the most important thing they had to do was to make good music, record good music and go out and be stars.'

In their turn, the Modern Lovers felt that Thau was too forceful for them. With the relationship not gelling, and after months now of similar failures, it was beginning to look as if the search for the 'perfect manager' was to be an impossible one (as that for the 'perfect record company' had been). In Ernie Brooks's words, such a person would have had to be 'a philosopher, a poet, the most honest person in the world and a good businessman' – and people with that particular combination of qualifications were pretty thin on the ground. As a result of the Modern Lovers' perfectionism, the opportunity to take on someone of lesser talents who might, nevertheless, have been effective enough was passed up.

On the other side of the equation, Thau had seen the single-minded vision and the stubbornness in Jonathan that, combined, were a major record company's worst nightmare and had felt that they were impossible to deal with on a commercial level. For Warner Brothers, the warning signs were flashing.

In the autumn of 1972, an incident occurred which, despite being a tragedy in itself, also abruptly terminated the band's idyll in Cohasset and, spell-like, seemed to contribute towards their downfall. Miss Christine, a member, along with John Cale's then wife, of Frank Zappa's groupie band Girls Together Outrageously (a.k.a. the GTOs), was staying at the house in Cohasset. She had arrived from Los Angeles, a visitor from another world as far as the band were concerned but familiar to Kim Fowley. 'The fact that I knew her made me OK. I think that the whole band had a crush on her, that she was the ultimate woman.' Lenny Kaye had met her, too, and recalls her being very different from the image shared by the GTOs. 'She was a lovely, lovely person . . . I remember her being somewhat akin to an angel.' The morning after she arrived she was found dead, having overdosed on a cocktail of prescription drugs. Whether she had chosen the band's house as a place to die or, as has been suggested, as the scene of a last attempt to save herself, with their help, was unclear.

She had arrived at the house with a pharmacopoeia of drugs, having told a few intimate friends (who may well not have believed her) that she was coming to Boston with the intention of killing herself – although the band did not find this out until later. John Felice and David Robinson spent the night talking to her and a girlfriend, with no hint that anything was amiss, finally calling a halt at six o'clock the next morning. When John woke at eleven a medical unit was making vain attempts to resuscitate her – apparently she had already been dead for some time.

Cohasset is a small town and the Modern Lovers' mansion was in the middle of a rich, exclusive community, intolerant of rock and roll at the best of times. The band had promised, on signing the lease, that there would be no drugs in the house. Three days later they were thrown out.

For an outfit whose rock-and-roll credo took a lot of its strength from rejection of drugs this incident undermined their self-confidence and the stance they had taken in a devastating and bitterly ironic way. Their stay in paradise was over and the impression began to seep into their minds now that their mission had been corrupted and that their vision might no longer be pure. Ernie believes that this incident 'somehow . . . psychologically destroyed us', and John considers that 'everything went into a tailspin' afterwards. In John's eyes, although the effects were felt by the whole band, it was Jonathan who seemed most affected: 'He seemed completely freaked out. He became very quiet; it was hard to say exactly what was going through his mind. He didn't want to talk about it at all.'

After a period without anywhere permanent to live, Jerry, John and David found a house in Arlington, north Boston, and Ernie, after staying for a while in an apartment in Cambridge, moved in with them.

Jonathan had always hoped to isolate the positive elements from those that were negative in rock and roll but now had witnessed something that indicated that this might not be possible without a deliberate move away from its centre. Over the coming months such a departure would come to seem more and more necessary.

At a gig in Radcliffe on 27 October the Modern Lovers played 'I'm Dropping My Friends One by One' ('Because I Would Rather Be Alone') – an upbeat tempo and jaunty tune concealing a retreat into solitude. They also played 'I Know I Turn Her On', its bitter/proud lyric set to a basic two-chord thrash augmented by a minor key, tight rhythm changes and howling lead guitar. During 'Hospital' Jonathan left long pauses between his opening lines, savouring the silence. The hall, sparsely attended on this night, with footsteps echoing across the floor in some of the quieter moments, had plenty of that. 'Astral Plane' sought a resolution for being lost in time ('it's been hard these past five thousand years'), and 'A Plea for Tenderness' called up Jonathan's father, mimicking his deep voice ('Son, she's confused, but she's very nice'). By the end of the latter Jonathan was singing far away from the microphone, still audible though, over the now muted sound of the band. This communication without amplification immediately established a very personal relationship with an audience – an approach that would increasingly attract him now but one that would increasingly estrange the other members of the band.

On New Year's Eve 1972 the Modern Lovers made a rare New York appearance (one of only three public performances the original band ever made there) supporting the New York Dolls at the Mercer Arts Center on Mercer Street. The 'Mercers' was a small complex of rooms initially intended for theatrical performances which also came to be used for rock-and-roll gigs, principally by the Dolls. (While the Modern Lovers were in New York on this occasion the two bands got together for a short recording session: with Jonathan and David Johansen on vocals, Johnny Thunders on guitar, Ernie on bass and David on drums, they taped a version of '96 Tears'.) Also on the bill were Suicide and Wayne County – a glittering line-up of proto-punk stars that overflowed into the audience, where Richard Hell was watching. 'Jonathan was one of the few interesting people around at that time. I remember the show at the Mercer Arts Center. It was basically the Dolls' crowd, really hysterical, very campy. Lots of gorgeous young girls, too, all in miniskirts and platforms and feather boas with heavy make-up.'

The Modern Lovers were eventually to get on stage at three thirty Their van had broken down in Hartford, Connecticut, on the way up from Boston and Ernie, who had been driving, had been forced to find a new starter motor. Because it was New Year's Eve the garage he found was busy bringing in the smashed-up cars of drunken drivers, and the wait was a long one.

While David Robinson was hanging around back in New York, he checked out the Mercers and found himself in a darkened room lit only by a few stage lights. On the stage were Suicide, and he was the only person in the audience. David was unsure if this was even a proper show but relished the performance the band proceeded to give, which even then was fully formed, looking and sounding like those they would go on to make in the mid- to late seventies.

The Modern Lovers, as a support band, had a set necessarily abbreviated from their usual length, but they managed to include some of their more reflective songs: 'Hospital' as well as 'She Cracked', 'A Plea for Tenderness' as well as 'Roadrunner'. The audience's reaction was a mixture of bemusement, derision, amusement and bliss.

After the MC's screeching, enthusiastic introduction, Jonathan, dressed, as noted by Judy Nylon in the *New Musical Express*, in 'penny-loafers and white sox, white T-shirt and chino sta-press jeans', made his own opening statement, his preface to 'Someone I Care About' implicitly drawing a cultural distinction between New York and Boston, before the band launched into their first attempt to win over this most hard-bitten of audiences.

Crowd pleasing, although certainly a consideration, was not to be allowed to water down the Modern Lovers' spirit or message. In case anyone missed it in the song itself, 'Dignified and Old', which followed 'Someone I Care About', had its essence put in a New York nutshell beforehand. Hysterical laughter initially greeted this introduction but then abruptly ceased. 'She Cracked' featured an extended one-chord rhythm guitar assault at its heart that must have had some of the audience convinced that they were witnessing the rebirth of the Velvet Underground. 'Old World' ('I'll never forget the past . . . I love the ancient ways') was followed by 'Hospital', the verses punctuated by a mixture of laughter and applause. Barracking was met by 'I don't care', and that was met by more applause, summing up the mixture of antagonism and appreciation that the band were arousing. Jonathan's sonic instructions for 'Astral Plane' consisted of 'Let's just turn this PA up a little, OK?' and various cries to the band of 'Way down!' The overall sound had to be loud enough, but the band on occasion quiet enough, for his lyrics to receive full attention. 'A Plea for Tenderness', the penultimate song, was always going to rely in this environment on the interest and goodwill built up through the rest of the set. A vital part of the Modern Lovers' overall message, there was no way the song was going to be sacrificed to any worries that it might not be understood. Jonathan's introduction was accompanied by an extended bout of tuning ('Thank you for being patient with us – it'll be worth it, though'), and the song was punctuated by tiny fragments of abuse from the audience that only pushed Jonathan deeper into intensity about its subject: 'You can't scare a man who's praying for you now.' Jonathan's delivery became more and more impassioned with the progress of the song, his voice breaking into falsetto, tears appearing in his eyes and shuddering through his words – he was living a rawness of emotion that a potentially unwilling audience simply had to acknowledge. He stopped playing and stood, beating on his chest, crying with emotion. The audience was stunned. New York, in all its thrashing variety, had never prepared them for this.

This was the moment of triumph. The Modern Lovers had come from Boston to New York and swayed that most cynical of audiences with a combination of prescient punk rock, beauty and the rawest and purest of emotions. The final surge through 'Roadrunner' was a celebration – some two-chord, high-speed rock and roll and a different kind of intensity.

The farewell message was: 'We're the Modern Lovers; we'll see you some other time.' The 'other time', however, would see the band in very different circumstances.

Although the Modern Lovers were well on the way to achieving their aims early in the New Year, and they still had the record company interest, the critical standing and the audience support to facilitate that achievement, it would also find them with an increasingly ominous feeling that their enterprise was now ill-starred.

# 4 A PLEA FOR TENDERNESS

DAVID Berson, on behalf of Warner Brothers, finally signed the Modern Lovers early in 1973, agreeing that John Cale would produce their début album, which was to be recorded in Los Angeles.

In an effort to fill the still vacant position of manager, Cale and Berson began boosting the band's image with 'pretty much every management company in America', as Cale puts it, and then Warner Brothers flew a selection of candidates (some of whom had already expressed interest in the Modern Lovers), together with their own representatives, to Boston to see them open for Aerosmith.

Owing to an administrative mix-up, at the time that the Modern Lovers took the stage the managers, who were all staying at the same hotel, were out having dinner and missed the set completely. Undaunted, the band invited them back to their house in Arlington, the large basement of which they used as rehearsal space. David Robinson's father, who owned a liquor store, provided the drinks, the Modern Lovers brought some friends along for atmosphere and here they recreated their live set. David Berson remembers it being 'terrific . . . another fabulous performance'.

After the show the band quizzed the managers extensively. Berson had tried to get them to concentrate on money, but their priorities were different and they chose other subjects instead – such as what books the managers read – in an effort to discover someone with concerns parallel to their own. No one made the grade.

By this time John Felice had again left the band, this time for good. For him, the gig with the New York Dolls had crystallized what he wanted to achieve musically – and he wanted to do it by getting his own band, the Real Kids, off the ground. For him, too, the atmosphere in the Modern Lovers was no longer what it used to be; he remembers an inability to agree, sometimes a 'stone silence at rehearsals' and a frustration born of what by now had been the breakdown of several sets of negotiations with managers and record companies. John was not happy either with the prospective trip to California, never having cared much for the West Coast, and felt that at the age of seventeen, having been 'hanging round some pretty crazy people' all of whom were older than him, it was time to embark on a career that was of his own making.

In the spring the Modern Lovers accepted an offer from a Harvard friend who was musical director of the Inverurie Hotel in Bermuda to play a residency there. They ended up staying at the Inverurie for about three weeks on what was really no more than a paid vacation, playing sets between the Esso Steel Band and the Fiery Limbo Dancers to an audience made up in part of waitresses, waiters and young people staying at the hotel but mainly of middle-aged tourists, to whom their act did not exactly endear them. These tourists were on holiday to relax and, having paid for the escapism of a 'show', they did not expect to be presented with the rather different appeal of the Modern Lovers. Many of them walked out in horror and the band's sets became shorter and shorter, evening by evening.

In an effort to appease the upset tourists the band went to the lengths of interjecting a couple of cover versions of Rolling Stones songs, one of which was 'Brown Sugar', into their set – but even this drastic measure failed. The fact that they managed to continue playing up until the end of the agreed period without being fired still fills them with wonder.

All four members of the band were living together in one room – something of a struggle since they often got on each other's nerves just living in the same house. To make matters worse Jonathan would sometimes refuse to leave the room and seemed extremely uptight. At a time when there was an undercurrent of unease anyway, more cracks were starting to appear in what had been a solid, focused unit. Another factor that would contribute toward the band's increasing disunity was Jonathan's first proper exposure to calypso, the musical style on which he would later base songs like 'Here Come the Martian Martians'. Jonathan had fallen in love with this music and was particularly taken with a band called the Bermuda Strollers, an experience he would later document in 'Down in Bermuda' from *Rockin' and Romance* and 'Monologue About Bermuda' from *Having a Party with Jonathan Richman*. For him, the vibrancy and joy that he found in this music, together with the continuing loosening-up that he was undergoing in his personal attitudes and relationships, meant that he saw a new era developing in his life. Although still espousing the same values he wanted to present them in a less confrontational manner, looking primarily to entertain as he did so.

What the rest of the band wanted, though, was to stay with the music that they loved, music which had given them a unique purpose and direction and to which they had devoted the last two years. For them, the fire was still there, and the possibility that all they had worked for might be wasted and that their potential careers might be slipping away from them, too, made them not a little frustrated and bitter. The thought that their music might develop in other directions later on was not necessarily anathema to them but, as they saw it, the immediate necessity was to concentrate on their current material and the prospect of recording it with John Cale for their first album.

Fortunately, on their return to Boston, this attitude prevailed, and the band found some much-needed collective enthusiasm for the upcoming sessions. Before leaving for California Jonathan was interviewed by Scott Cohen (who would later reprise the Modern Lovers' history in *Spin* magazine) for the New York-based *Andy Warhol's Interview*. This was a fascinating run-through of Jonathan's ideas on 'Modern Love' and its relation to sex, his 'dream date', his approach to song-writing, the putting across of his message at live shows, personal heroes and much more. Here he looked forward to California because it would be a new experience and he wanted to record as soon as possible. This interview was also the source of his much-quoted hopes that everyone could 'get along better with dogs and cats because that would help us to get along better with people' and that the band would play softer 'because I believe that any group that would hurt the ears of infants – and this is no joke – sucks'. There was plenty of optimism here for the band's future, but it was very much a future on Jonathan's own terms, and those terms were as much a departure from the past as they were a continuation of it.

By the summer, the Modern Lovers were driving to California with the intention of making an album that would document and build on their achievements, an album that would live up there with the very best.

Los Angeles was hot, seemingly full of record business employees on the make and peppered with people living lifestyles based on a distorted image of the West Coast in the late sixties. The band's fleeting visit the year before had not gone far towards giving the Modern Lovers an idea of what it was like actually to live there. Not only was the climate very different and hard to adjust to (surprisingly, given his later move to California, it was Jonathan who was most affected by this) but all the things they despised were not merely around, they were embedded in the culture. Boston, despite its conservatism, had an East Coast realism which they understood and worked within. Here, realism was what made you turn the screw on the other guy when you were doing business with him, otherwise it was out of the window.

Night life in California was also very different to that in Boston. The clubs on Sunset Boulevard and Hollywood Boulevard, such as Rodney Bingenheimer's English Disco, were frequented by girls from the Valley and the Strip and the scene was centred on a West Coast imitation of the New York Dolls with platform shoes everywhere. Ernie and Jerry gazed on all this artifice with a mixture of disdain and fascination – it was like a distorted mirror image of their own world. As such it was not a world they could really have entered even if they had wanted to. Ernie readily admits that they regarded themselves as too 'sophisticated', whereas the natives, for their part, regarded these displaced East Coasters as too 'square'.

For Warner Brothers the recording of the projected album in Los Angeles meant that they could keep a close eye on a band that still had no other form of management and was, in many ways, pretty disorganized. This close attention, however, was another pressure on the band who, their newly restored solidarity already weakening once more, were having plenty of problems with the existing ones. Jonathan, in particular, soon started to resent what he saw as the record company's interference, disallowing as it did his usual detachment from business, and before long his disaffection would manifest itself in an unwillingness to co-operate. Over the course of the summer the band gigged in California. As well as the notorious 'Warners showcase' with Tower of Power at San Bernardino, mentioned earlier, they played again at the Long Branch Saloon, Berkeley. Here, the band renewed their acquaintance with Matthew Kaufman – and borrowed equipment from one of his bands, Earthquake. Kaufman, in turn, renewed his offer of management and, even though it was again declined, noted the strain in the band, making it clear to Jonathan that the offer would still apply were he to become a solo artist.

A look at the set-list gives little indication that there had been any change of direction since the Modern Lovers' early days – still present were songs that had created and reflected their identity, songs such as 'Pablo Picasso', 'Modern World' and 'I'm Straight'. Their presentation, however, when the band hit the stage, would tell a different story.

As a warm-up Jonathan performed a near-solo rendition (accompanied only by a little bass from Ernie) of 'Boston Boston USA', a semi-serious celebration of his home town. Afterwards, while the band tuned, Jonathan bantered good-humouredly with the audience before launching into 'Louie Louie' accompanied by bass and then finally by drums – at which point it collapsed. 'Modern World' and 'She Cracked', although less frenetic than of old, seemed to have been revitalized by the introduction of new lyrics, and 'Pablo Picasso', complete with spoken introduction, rearranged instrumentation and 'New York subway feeling' for a rumbling rhythm guitar solo, was streamlined but authentic until it neared its end, when Jonathan, sounding bored, took to playing with the melody of the vocal line, misshaping it and taking it away from the heart of the song. A new composition, 'Falling in Love Must Be Two Ways', was delivered with passion. Its setting was restrained, backed initially only by Jonathan's rhythm guitar, which was then joined by bass and finally tambourine. The audience loved it, clapping to the beat, and Jonathan responded by turning up the volume for a deft and triumphant rhythm guitar solo. 'Don't Let Our Youth Go to Waste', though, a song that demands deliberation, was hustled out of existence here. Strangely brisk as it began, its pace only increased – Jonathan seemed embarrassed by it and, by the end, its potency was a thing of the past. Similarly, the version of 'Someone I Care About' was everything it should not be. Easy-paced and slightly perfunctory, it was also abbreviated and, with Jonathan sometimes accompanied only by bass and drums, it no longer had the impact necessary to tear through the prejudices of an audience. More suited to the new, pared-down Modern Lovers sound was 'A Plea for Tenderness', and Jonathan enjoyed the chance it gave to improvise lyrics and to sing something that said more about his current state of mind than the songs that had been written three and four years ago. 'I'm Straight' by now lacked the dynamics of its earlier incarnations – 'Hippy Johnny' was 'a nice guy', although 'always stoned' – but there was still some passion here, with Jonathan 'proud' to shout and repeat the song's message. One chord and the band were into 'Roadrunner' – straight-forward and rocking, it provided a classic Modern Lovers finale.

It had been a good-humoured performance, but there had been times when Jonathan seemed to lack what, to him, was absolutely vital – commitment to what he was singing. There had been plenty of classic Modern Lovers material; some songs had been reinterpreted and were apparently looking to the future, but others, their delivery lacking the old passion, had had their power drained away.

Jonathan's guitar-playing had given many examples of his continuing abilities as an electric guitarist in a style that was still reminiscent of Lou Reed, but then it had also dispensed with distortion and reined in the volume to the extent that the whole sound of the band seemed to be changing.

In short, while there were sufficient indications that the Modern Lovers had a future, there were also ominous signs that compromise would be needed if they were to avoid being consigned to the past.

Warner Brothers had rented a house for the band on Kings Road, just north of the Continental Hyatt House, in Van Nuys, a suburb of Los Angeles (the house where Emmylou Harris, who was working with Gram Parsons at the time, had previously been living). Here Jonathan's room contained a mattress, some dirty clothes, a guitar and a baseball glove.

Gram Parsons had a cabin out in the Valley and the Modern Lovers soon got to know him – they would go and visit him there and sometimes play guitar together (there was also talk of a more formal musical collaboration, but this was an idea that, sadly, with tragedy just around the corner, would never be allowed to reach fruition). They regularly played in the same softball games – Ernie even remembers a particularly drunk Parsons attempting miniature golf. The Modern Lovers also visited him at the larger house just in front of his that belonged to Phil Kaufman. Kaufman was Parsons's road manager (he had also worked in this capacity for the Rolling Stones) and had been recently taken on by Warners to do the same job for the Modern Lovers.

Phil Kaufman's partner and long-time friend was Eddie Tickner, original manager of the Byrds. Older than most of the other people around that scene and 'a good manager, a gentleman', in Kim Fowley's words, he now agreed, when asked by Warner Brothers, to take temporary charge of the Modern Lovers, having been one of the managers flown out to Boston by the record company the previous year. Although there was a general sense of relief that a management team had now been installed, it was something that should have been done much earlier if it was to have had any real effect.

Warner Brothers were anxious to get the Modern Lovers back into the studio so that they could finally record the album that had been so long in the making. John Cale was also keen to get moving. He had good memories of the short time the previous year when he had worked with the band and was looking forward to the chance to improve on those demos and to make the unique record that would fulfil their potential. This new session would be taped at Elektra Studios, where Cale had produced the first Stooges album. The Modern Lovers were delighted to find that the oriental rug from the cover of that record was still in place on the floor there.

While Cale wanted to take the confrontational energy that he remembered and push it a stage further, Jonathan was now single-mindedly heading in the opposite direction. He wanted to reduce the instrumentation and the volume and had already changed some of his lyrics in order to smooth down what he saw as their harsh edges. Some songs he wanted dropped altogether and replaced with his newer material. By now these older songs had been played so many times that it was getting progressively harder to recapture the power of their early performances, and Jonathan was railing more and more against what he saw as the increasing artificiality of the process. Once in the studio all this was put into starker relief as Cale tried to draw anger out of him, telling him to attack what he was singing, and Jonathan replied that he didn't feel anger and would not and could not fake it.

As well as this, the pressure was still there to make *the* album. There was also the nagging thought that perhaps this music was never intended to be captured within the confines of a studio – that perhaps the magic only really occurred within the unpredictability of a live setting. All this was enough to stretch the relationship between band and producer to breaking point. Cale remembers the sessions as being 'like Catch-22 at every turn . . . every complaint about how things were sounding or which direction they were going was countered with another complaint. It was a never-ending spiral that seemed to be very destructive . . . I kind of felt bad for [Jonathan], because it was directionless. It was just rehearsed to death – that's not the way. It was picking at sores after a while . . . At the end, he didn't trust me and I don't know why, something happened, and that broke it with me. I thought: I don't know why this is happening, but it's painful. I'm going to leave . . . It was a shame, because I felt that there was such an innocence that was worth capturing, that was kind of unbelievable in a way. Nobody believed that these guys were writing songs about government centres . . . What happened basically was that Jonathan had success that he didn't want. As soon as that contract was signed something happened that altered his view of record making, and he became very contrary.'

The sessions were terminated this time before a single song had been completed, and the future was now beginning to look decidedly bleak for the Modern Lovers. With the benefit of hindsight the quick-fire session of the previous year had probably been the ideal way to record them, but that was still regarded as merely a demo.

Danny Fields remembers being on a Warner Brothers jet with chairman Mo Ostin as they flew down to Memphis to see the Doobie Brothers play. Having arrived and listened to the first few songs of the band's set the visitors decided that, actually, what they really wanted to do was to return to New York – as fast as they could. Mo hired a special boat and before long they were speeding along the Mississippi towards the riverside limousines that were waiting to take them back to the airport. Once they got there, although it was now the early hours of the morning, a jet had already been prepared that would see them in the Big Apple again by sunrise. By the time they touched down back home Danny had spent the whole trip – both legs of it – hounding Ostin and trying in vain to persuade him to release the 1972 Cale session as an album, because 'this was the greatest band of all time'.

John Cale was the main reason the Modern Lovers had signed for Warner Brothers in the first place. With him no longer a part of the equation the other pressures on them started to squeeze even more.

At this point, Kim Fowley again appeared on the scene. He had been enlisted by Warner Brothers as someone who knew the band and who would be well placed to intercede successfully between artists and record company and to come up with some saleable product. By this stage Warner Brothers could see all too clearly the prospect of their investment going up in smoke, and they were desperate to find someone who could maybe dampen down the flames long enough to get an album out and promoted. The band, having recorded with Fowley before, were happy with the arrangement and agreed to try again, this time at the 24-track Gold Star studios in Los Angeles, where Phil Spector had produced his most important work.

Although a lot of money had already been spent it was agreed that Fowley would begin from scratch rather than attempt to fill the holes in the work that Cale had already done. His engineer would be Stan Ross, who had already worked on records by the Beach Boys, Buffalo Springfield and the Who.

Fowley went up to the band's house in Van Nuys where they had their own soundproof rehearsal room and listened to them go through their songs again. Many were, of course, familiar to him from the Dinky Dawson session the previous year, but, although the material may have been similar, Fowley quickly noticed changes in the band. He could now see real friction between Jonathan and the others.

When the time came for the actual recording Fowley remembers Jonathan insisting that everyone on the production side hide under the console, while he recorded his vocals in the dark. On one occasion, too, Phil Kaufman remembers Fowley instructing him to lock the band in the studio and not give them food or drink until they had a particular take. 'They were whining, but I wouldn't let them out.' Jerry played a little guitar at these sessions as well as keyboards and, he explains why he had recently taken up the instrument: 'I'd got kind of frustrated because Jonathan had switched to a new style of guitar that didn't use much distortion, so I sometimes played some of his old parts. He gave me a Telecaster that he no longer liked. I used that. He'd still play, but kind of as he does now, little Chuck Berry riffs, generally a far cleaner sound. There's like the great divide in Jonathan's guitar-playing between the time when he's trying to emulate Sterling Morrison and Lou Reed and when he decided that he did like Chuck Berry – up until that time he hated Chuck Berry.'

Surprisingly, recording went fairly smoothly, with little of the bitterness that had characterized the Cale sessions. Jonathan seemed to be resigned to the idea of putting these old songs to rest once and for all, but his waning enthusiasm for them meant that he was not always able to do it with sincerity and, on occasion, found himself going through the motions – something totally contrary to his instincts. On the other hand, he was able to record some of his newer material as well – and there was some satisfaction to be had in that.

The old songs that the band played included 'She Cracked', 'Modern World', 'Girlfriend' and 'Roadrunner'. Of these, the first two, in particular, unexpectedly pack a real punch.

The version of 'She Cracked' is lyrically much less harsh than the original. The contrasts are reduced. Self-hate is replaced by an attempt to understand the girl's behaviour and to help her, and the first two-thirds of the song are now generalized, rather than specific. The song's middle-eight is a burst of multi-channel radio interference; the drums are crisp, bass urgent, rhythm guitar abrupt and sharp, keyboards vibrant with distortion. Occasionally the vocals are garbled or twisted into odd shapes, and, occasionally, the old passion seeps through. The messages flowing from this version of the song and this performance of it reveal a pivotal moment in the band's history. 'Modern World' is slowed down from the take on the Appere/Mason session and, like 'She Cracked', features a redirected lyric. In the original version love could counteract the power of the worst elements of the modern world and make the best parts transcendent – it was a question of getting the distinction right and unifying the vision. In this version, the worst parts (and, with no attempt to run away from the truth – they're as bad as ever, if not worse) are no longer to be confronted. The hope now is of a helpful coexistence – an attempt to improve from within rather than from the outside. At one point during this performance, Jonathan, a rather bitter tongue in his cheek, says: 'Keep angry and tough, everybody,/We'll stick it out', and the song, after a guitar/keyboard battle as frenetic and passionate as those of the preceding year, ends in his laughter.

Apart from the old songs, other material recorded at Gold Star included 'Yea, Pretty Life' (no version of this has yet surfaced), 'Falling in Love Must Be Two Ways', 'I Wanna Sleep in Your Arms', 'Government Center' and 'Fly into the Mystery'.

'Fly into the Mystery', which Jonathan would later re-record for *Rock and Roll with the Modern Lovers*, had already been a part of the band's live set for a long time, and Jonathan would sometimes introduce it as 'the Modern Lovers' slow dance number'. Here the setting of the song features ethereal backing vocals and keyboard overdubs appropriate to its rather stately grandeur. At eight o'clock on a starlit night the Boston stores, Farleine's and Gilchrist's, have just closed and the mystery of Beverly, on Boston's north shore, is only a short drive away. The mystery is where Jonathan takes his girlfriend when they want to dream together and it's also where a boy can go to dream alone when his girl has deserted him, intent on flying into a different mystery. ('Fly into the Mystery' also had a companion piece, no proper recorded version of which survives, called 'New England Summer Song'. With similar themes of the magic of nature and romance, it is also a more generalized slice of the variety of New England life set to a a melody enhanced by keyboard trills and driving rhythm guitar.)

'I Wanna Sleep in Your Arms' is a polar opposite to 'Fly into the Mystery', a frenetic plea for love and an end to uptight loneliness set to a variation on Iggy Pop's 'I Got a Right'. (Iggy was one of the band's long-time heroes and their paths crossed briefly a few times. During their stay in California, Ernie and Jerry met him at one of his shows at the Whisky a Go Go in Los Angeles, and he proudly pulled up his shirt and showed them the scars on his chest from a recent self-mutilation with a bottle at Max's Kansas City.) There is a passion and a tautness in this version of 'I Wanna Sleep in Your Arms' that is hard to equate with the imminent dissolution of the band. Both Jonathan's vocal performance and his guitar work demonstrate a genuine sense of commitment, with a frantic but measured treble-high rhythm break. There is a twin guitar propulsion here, too – Jerry making one of his new appearances away from the keyboard – and, with both guitarists playing rhythm, the song harnesses its power with absolute efficiency and certainty.

'Government Center' is the first sign of Jonathan's new direction and would later be re-recorded for the *Beserkley Chartbusters* album. There it would be joined by a cover version of 'It Will Stand', and the two songs express a shared belief in the power of rock and roll to transform lives. 'Government Center' gives it a mission to conquer boredom and the mundane and bring joy to people. Here, specifically, the people are those working in Boston's uninspiring office building of the title; built in an old part of Boston that had been torn down in the sixties, the development was a huge, open plaza, a 'windswept, cold, empty place', as David Robinson describes it, that people would pass through on their way in and out of offices – a bleak part of town. 'Government Center' has an appropriately sixties feel, with Farfisa organ, hand claps and an introduction courtesy of Tommy James and the Shandells' 'I Think We're Alone Now'. It works well, and the band get energetically behind it. It's the kind of piece that could have fitted into their past repertoire without too much of the join showing, and it is a fascinating indication, therefore, of what might have been.

The rest of the material recorded at the session is certainly not lacking in commitment and has plenty of power, with a tight and punchy drums/bass sound to propel it along. 'Hospital' opens and closes with a haunting organ melody and features some particularly beautiful and adept guitar-playing from Jonathan in the solo – the vocal performance, too, is full of feeling. The sum of these parts is a gorgeous melancholy. 'I'm Straight' lacks the bitterness of previous versions, with Jonathan reducing the personal finger-pointing – 'I like him, too, I like Hippy Johnny' – although he is still 'proud' to say that he's straight and wants the other Modern Lovers to 'tell the world'. Eerie organ and guitar 'percussion' from Jonathan, some of it using one-string harmonics, add distinction to what is a strong updating of a song that had been showing its age. 'A Plea for Tenderness' is nothing less than a *tour de force* – as close as it is possible to get to a creation of heightened emotion in a recording studio. A long spoken introduction backed only by occasional guitar chords gives way to a huge outpouring of desire and frustration in an attempt almost to wear down the girl at whom the song is directed. The band are repeatedly given instructions: 'Tell me now . . . I want to hear you scream it . . . Louder . . . Help me out . . . Way down, men . . .' in an attempt to enlist their power in the way most likely to achieve success for Jonathan's case (the song's 'narrator' is theoretically anonymous, but there is no doubt that every word and nuance is his). Throughout the song you can hear Jonathan's breathing in the gaps between sentences and in the pauses as he tries to express his feelings exactly – much of what is going on here is improvised – and there is even a gulp for air that is almost a stifled sob.

In attendance at these Gold Star sessions was Gram Parsons. The Modern Lovers had visited him while he recorded his *Return of the Grievous Angel* album and were now returning his hospitality. Kim Fowley remembers this unlikely friendship. 'Gram Parsons came to the sessions . . . he liked those guys, I was surprised because he was such a macho guy, with his drinking and drugging, but he actually liked their music and thought it was good. Jonathan Richman and the boys were worshipped by Gram Parsons, and they worshipped him back.'

It was not long after this that Parsons made his drug-fuelled visit to the motel where he would die tragically the next day of an over-dose. In common with his other friends, the Modern Lovers had sensed a self-destructive frame of mind in him that day. Although they had only known him for a short while Parsons had become a friend (he had even come to their aid when things had looked like getting out of hand backstage at the Tower of Power gig), and the Modern Lovers were deeply upset by his death. There were also echoes here of Miss Christine's death the previous year and all the anguish that that had caused – for something similar to happen around the band so soon after, and at a time when they were feeling beleaguered, was another body blow to what were, by now, already bleak prospects.

Parsons was due to be buried in his home town of Jacksonville, Florida, but Phil Kaufman, feeling that this was not what he would have wanted, took his body instead out to the Joshua Tree National Monument in the desert, where he tried to cremate it. The remains were found and Kaufman was arrested on his return home from a day's recording with the Modern Lovers.

'I got arrested for stealing Gram's body. I left the studio on my motor-cycle, my old Harley, and came back to this. They never charged us with stealing the body; they just charged us with stealing the coffin.' Kaufman had previously been in prison with Charles Manson, and the press could not believe their luck. They went to town on the story and ensured plenty of publicity during the court case.

The result of this hearing was a $1,300 fine. Needing to raise funds to pay it, Kaufman arranged a benefit gig – 'Kaufman's Koffin Kaper Konsert' – in the back yard of his house. The Modern Lovers were asked to play at this event and duly did so, along with Bobby 'Boris' Pickett and the Cryptkickers of 'Monster Mash' fame. Kaufman describes the event as 'a pot-pourri of eclectic nonsense' with 'food, beer and loud music'. Lowell George of Little Feat, whom he had known well since their days together at Hollywood High, came along as did other members of the local music business. Nudie Cohen (rodeo tailor to Gram Parsons and the Flying Burrito Brothers, among others) contributed five hundred dollars, and enough money was made to pay the fine.

Despite what could have been regarded as at least a partial success in the recording studio with Fowley, time was fast running out for the Modern Lovers. Jonathan had agreed to the Fowley sessions, but he had made it clear to the band, in private, that recording the old songs was one thing but playing them live was another. For their part Ernie and Jerry were willing to compromise and perform a live set that was a mixture of the old and the new and tried to invoke the original spirit of the band and its common cause in an attempt to persuade Jonathan to reconsider.

When David Berson rang the house in Van Nuys and Jonathan

answered, there was no way he could lie to the direct questions he was asked about the band's future. He made it clear that he would not be able to play the songs that would form the basis of their début album in any live performance to promote it. David Berson had been trying to keep the band together, against increasing odds, for some time – calling on Phil Kaufman, Eddie Tickner and anyone else with an influence to help – and he was a long-standing admirer and personal friend of the band (they had even driven out to Scranton, Pennsylvania, that summer to play at his wedding), but this was impossible to countenance. An album that could not be promoted was, for a huge corporation like Warner Brothers, commercial suicide and, no matter how deep Berson's love for the band, such an album could never be allowed a release. Warner Brothers withdrew its support from the Modern Lovers, including the use of the house in Van Nuys, and, after three months in California, they were stranded.

In December 1973 they returned dispiritedly to Boston – except Jonathan who remained for a while on his own. For David, the end of their three months in California was not just deeply depressing, it was the final straw, and he quit the band. The loss of David was another disaster for any lingering hope that was left for the Modern Lovers. However, even without him Jerry and Ernie believed there was still enough of the band's essence left for them to be able to re-create some of the original magic. They approached an old friend from Harvard called Bob Turner and, in an attempt to keep going despite everything, asked him to fill the vacant drummer's position.

The distance they would have had to travel to accommodate Jonathan's new ideas into a viable new approach can be seen by a look at a studio acetate from around this time featuring a series of solo performances from Jonathan. Accompanied by alternating acoustic guitar, tambourine and maracas, all played by himself, and sometimes by nothing at all apart from the slapping of his thighs, Jonathan runs through some recent Modern Lovers songs ('Song of Remembrance for Old Girlfriends ', 'Hey There Little Insect', and 'Falling in Love Must Be Two Ways'), three cover versions (including 'Crazy Little Mama') and a host of totally new songs, some semi-improvised. Ernie and Jerry, although expected, as this excerpt from the conversation between the songs shows, never arrived. 'I actually worry about Ernie and Jerry. I hope they can get in, but I don't know what they're really doing. Maybe we should . . . well, obviously they realize that I've got the key here, they'll realize it by now, if they didn't.'

'Falling in Love Must Be Two Ways' is all about the necessity for love to be reciprocated for it to achieve its true meaning. Anticipating some of his later 'persuasive/argumentative' love songs this late Modern Lovers number, melodic and refusing bitterness, is an indication of Jonathan's changing lyrical approach.

Of the new songs, 'Veil of Cold' and 'I Feel Alright' are almost like mantras, with lines repeated over and over again. Pleas for his love to be accepted and returned, it is almost as if Jonathan believes (as in 'A Plea for Tenderness') that insistence and conviction can themselves bring about the fruition of his desire. 'Awkward Love' is an extraordinary statement of intent: not only will Jonathan wait for the fruition of his love ('awkward', yes, but also true and therefore destined to achieve fruition), he will wait with compassion, putting up with his girl's other boyfriends, resisting the pain of loneliness in the expectation of eventual success. The intensity and self-willed certainty are almost shocking but, in his later life with his future wife Gail, about whom these songs were written (and many others would later be written), his certainty would be affirmed.

Jonathan had first met Gail a few months earlier at a Modern Lovers gig in Ipswich. Although by then he had already noticed her in the audience, that night was the first occasion he had ever heard her voice, shouting the words 'We love you' at the band during the course of the show. Jonathan had sensed straight away that she was the one for him, and after meeting her fell in love with her. However, it was to be another four years – in which period her first marriage would have produced a son – before he would succeed in winning her over to him. During this time their only contact came from his intermittent letters and telephone calls. Despite the initial lack of reciprocation of his feelings, he continued to write songs for her and to try through them to will his love into her mind.

On the acetate, an unaccompanied version of the Lovin' Spoonful's 'Do You Believe in Magic?' is followed by an exposition of Jonathan's new, John Cage-like musical philosophy: 'Look, let's just share all of these found objects . . . picking up the first thing . . . look how great everything works, and we'll do it everywhere, see . . . so you're not restricted to a club, because you don't need to play with anything, almost every place has chairs, even outside, you can play on anything . . . now it's OK . . . I know what it sounds like, it sounds just like me.'

Whether this approach could ever have been reconciled with a continuation of the Modern Lovers is an intriguing thought. Certainly it might have recaptured some of the old provocation and crusading spirit and, in so doing, it might just have brought the members closer together again, but, equally, the drastic change in style and content could well have been irreconcilable with Ernie's and Jerry's sensibilities. Either way, there was the potential for a fascinating collision.

For the time being, strange as it may seem, life carried on for the Modern Lovers. Although Warner Brothers had withdrawn financial support from them the band was still officially signed to the label. They decided to take on a new manager, Bob Aiss, who suggested that he arrange some gigs to show the record company that, although there had been changes both in personnel and in material, they were still a commercial prospect. On 26 and 27 January 1974 the Modern Lovers played at the Townhouse Theatre in New York.

While they had been away in California their standing on the East Coast had increased and they found themselves in the curious position of being on the verge of complete disintegration and at the same time more popular than they had ever been. At the Townhouse Jonathan insisted on the band playing at a much lower volume than ever before, an insistence that the others saw as another assertion of his own new vision at the expense of the one common to them all. (By this time Ernie was beginning to believe that there was an element of perversity in Jonathan's new attitude and maybe even, as John Cale suggested, a fear of success – although now, in retrospect, he is more inclined to see it as sincerity of vision.) Several of the new songs had been introduced by the time of the concerts, including 'Government Center' and 'Here We Are in Dreamland'. The band also played 'Hey There Little Insect', featuring Jerry and Ernie on backing vocals unenthusiastically singing 'Buzz buzz'. At one point, Jonathan instructed the band to leave the stage while he continued solo, beating time with his baseball glove.

A review in *Variety* certainly saw them very much as a going concern, although noting the contrast between Jonathan's quiet openings to the songs and the band's 'heavy rockin' sound' when the rest of them joined in. Jonathan, now sporting a moustache (there was also a brief flirtation with a beard around now) was 'wide-eyed and straight-faced', and the reviewer bizarrely managed to find 'banality' in his lyrics, wondering, consequently, whether this could ever allow the band to transcend their cult following. 'Their upcoming Warner Brothers Records discs could widen their fame. As of now, though, their performance has limited appeal.' Although badly informed as to the current state of play with the band, the reviewer's sense of unease about their future was to be all too quickly confirmed.

For David Berson at Warner Brothers there was to be no relaunch. As far as he was concerned, the band may have had the same name but their direction was now so different, and the contrast with their old approach so great, as to be unworkable.

In February the band played what was to be their last ever gig at a club called Sandy's in Beverly. By now Jonathan was unwilling to play 'Roadrunner' and the band had to struggle hard here to get him to change his mind, pointing out how much the people in the audience – many of whom were calling for it – really loved it.

The gig was received rapturously, but after the first set Jonathan informed Jerry that he was playing too loudly and that he couldn't hear himself sing. Jerry, who had thought that Jonathan's vocals were too loud, tried in vain to argue his point. Realizing that he was getting nowhere and that this was a point beyond which it was impossible to go, Jerry told Jonathan it was time for him to leave the band. Obliged to finish the show, however, they all continued with the second set and were rewarded with three encores, ending with an improvisation featuring Jonathan's attempts to explain his need for silence and how no one understood it. At the end of the gig Bob Turner also told Jonathan he had decided to quit and, although Ernie was not opposed to working with Jonathan again (and would do so the next year), the Modern Lovers effectively ceased to exist.

What should have been a long chapter in the history of rock and roll had tailed off after only a few pages. There were steps that could have been taken at almost every stage of the band's last year to prolong their existence and fulfil their potential, but, finally, they were overwhelmed by a suffocating accumulation of pressures that proved impossible to shrug off. In their integrity, their courage, their love, their ability to face and to tell the truth, their raw power, their intensity and their humour, the Modern Lovers have never been equalled.

Throughout the years since 1974 the band have not been forgotten. *The Modern Lovers* was released in 1976 to a rapturous reception and has been regularly re-released since then. Tracks from the Dinky Dawson and Gold Star sessions have appeared on legal and not-so-legal releases and, with the issuing of *Live at the Long Branch Saloon/Precise Modern Lovers Order*, there is at last a permanent record of their live performances. They were a profound influence on both British and American punk rock, and cover versions of their songs have been recorded by artists as diverse as John Cale, the Sex Pistols and Siouxsie and the Banshees and performed live by REM, Talking Heads and Alex Chilton, among others. More of their work will see the light of day and we will probably soon have as near complete a representation of them as is possible. As for the years they could have had and the impact they could have made if circumstances had been different, all that can be said is that they would have been both unique and momentous.

David moved on to The Pop, a punk band called DMZ and the Cars, John formed his own band, the Real Kids, and Jerry went on to play with Elliott Murphy, Talking Heads and his own band, the

Casual Gods. Ernie has played with Elliott Murphy, the Necessaries and David Johansen.

They have all met Jonathan recently and enjoyed the experience – in fact they are all getting on with him better than ever.

When asked about the prospect of the band getting together again, however, Jonathan finds other subjects more interesting.

# 5 HERE COME THE MARTIAN MARTIANS

For Jonathan the final disbanding of the Modern Lovers was another stage in his progress towards greater relaxation, personal freedom and a new way of seeing the world. All this would soon find an almost organic expression in his work, which would now embody purely his own vision, no longer constrained by what had become the conflicting viewpoints of the other band members and no longer bound by the commercial pressures of record companies and managers. On Jonathan's return to Boston, John Felice remembers a huge change in him: he was full of joy and 'almost reborn' – as if he was finally rid of a huge burden.

None of this meant that he would disown his past, however, and his new freedom was exactly that – it added to the range of choices available to him without taking anything away. When the chance came soon afterwards to record a Velvet Underground song with Moe Tucker (and to do the right song his way) he was happy to take it.

At the end of February 1974 Steve Sesnick, the former Velvet Underground manager, arranged for Moe to travel to Boston where a studio called Music Designers had been booked. Here, with stalwarts of the Boston scene Willie Alexander and Walter Powers (who had both briefly joined Moe in a post-Lou Reed Velvet Underground), a guitarist called George Nardo and drummer Jim Wilkins, they recorded a version of Lou Reed's 'I'm Sticking with You' (the Velvet Underground's version would not finally be released for another ten years). Jonathan and Moe sang the two lead vocal parts, Walter Powers played bass, and Willie Alexander contributed backing vocals and a 'cameo' vocal for the song's spoken bridge, replacing the original version's reference to 'soldiers fighting with the Cong' in the process. The recording, which was to be released as one side of a single, was essentially light-hearted and needs to be considered accordingly, but it is an affectionate performance – and a fascinating, if minor, piece of history.

Sesnick had also arranged a concert to coincide with the recording, again featuring Moe and Jonathan but, in the event, although she attended, Moe never played. Jonathan did – Moe's memories are of him 'beating on the stage with newspapers'.

Jonathan now started playing solo 'a few hospital shows for kids and an elementary school or two' (as he would later put it in his 'biography'). Although he had always brought his music to children these performances would now become more regular and play a bigger part in his musical and personal development. Here he would not only bring an acoustic guitar but also the new percussion Moe had seen him using. Jonathan wanted to involve these audiences in his shows, and the rolled-up newspapers that he brought with him were examples of the 'found' instruments he had already theorized about which could be played by anyone. He would bring them along to the schools and hospitals, and the children would use them to beat time to his songs, reflecting back their joy and building on it. This was the process Jonathan was interested in and the character of the children's response to him and the effects that he, in turn, felt would inform him of the extent of his success. The children who, like him, were uncluttered by preconceptions and cynicism would be part of a pure circuit of joy, feeding back into itself. Learning from this experience, Jonathan would later on be able to take it a stage further and bring the same material to adults, applying the lessons he had learned about the creation and reciprocation of joy. The idea was for the songs to appeal to a wider audience, not just a different one, and he wanted adults to be able to experience the same happiness and excitement as the children.

Staying on in California for a while after the return to Boston of the other members of the Modern Lovers, Jonathan had continued his long-standing policy of performing for disadvantaged children, as Phil Kaufman recalls: 'Jonathan and I would go out on weekends to hospitals for mentally handicapped children. I'd be carrying the amp and he'd set up. He'd really be able to communicate with them; he didn't see the disability. They loved him . . . It's really a unique gift that he has.'

The music business represented greed, drugs and negativity to Jonathan, and he now wanted to distance himself from it. His patience with some of the audiences it catered for had been exhausted, too, and he wanted his increasing positivism and joy at what the world could offer to bring him new listeners who could absorb and reflect those feelings. Although he would continue to play colleges and occasional other dates over the next two or three years (and certainly continue to be involved with rock music), the new audiences that he had found, in their unconventional environments, would see more live performances by him than traditional audiences in traditional venues. Here, and in this company, Jonathan would have room to breathe and to rejuvenate himself, firmly to establish his new outlook and his new way of life. His return to full-scale live gigs and record-making with a new band, when it did come, would be rooted in his radical rethinking and in the experience gained in these new 'theatres'.

Still living in Boston, he resided on the floor of his old friend John Felice who noticed a real excitement in him about the new material he was writing. Both Jonathan and John had recently taken steps to determine for themselves the directions of their careers and this, combined with their long-standing friendship, meant that they were particularly close.

Over the next few months, Jonathan would develop his new thinking in both his life and work. He was happy with his new freedom and relaxation and with his new self-determination.

Towards the end of 1974 he received a phone call from Berkeley, California: Matthew Kaufman had decided that the time was ripe to produce the first albums for his new record label and he wanted Jonathan to contribute four tracks to the unassumingly titled *Beserkley Chartbusters Volume One*, which would also feature Greg Kihn, the Rubinoos and Earthquake. Jonathan was rested, revitalized and keen to subject himself to a new challenge – and looking forward to enjoying himself in the process.

This was to be very much a rock-and-roll record, so, while being an opportunity to put some of his new ideas into practice, it would also allow Jonathan to assimilate them into what had gone before and to show that his new direction was the result of growth rather than uprooting.

Jonathan, looking forward to the opportunities for musical exploration that he might encounter on his trip, and confident that his new outlook could only grow in strength there, headed by train from East Coast to West and to a new temporary residence: a sofa in the house that doubled as the office of Beserkley Records.

In Berkeley Jonathan was to get plenty of opportunities for new musical experience. Perhaps the most bizarre, showing (as the recording of 'I'm Sticking with You' also had) that the changes he was undergoing had certainly not closed any doors to him, came soon after his arrival, when he met up with some fellow expatriate East Coasters. These were acquaintances from the early seventies Boston scene who had shared Jonathan's roots there in a love of both early rock and roll and the Velvet Underground, and who were now playing small clubs on the West Coast, as well as recently performing at the Whisky a Go Go. They were working with material and an approach arguably as far removed from that of the current rock music scene – particularly on the West Coast – as Jonathan's own and had a similar desire for single-minded pursuit of their artistic vision. Despite the fact that this vision had developed very differently from Jonathan's there was enough common ground between them, and enough desire for musical adventure on both sides, for Jonathan to be asked along to an audition night at the Fillmore West where he would find himself becoming the first ever drummer for the Patti Smith Group.

At this time, before the arrival of Ivan Kral, the group consisted of Patti Smith herself, Lenny Kaye on guitar and Richard Sohl on piano. Kaye recalls the occasion: 'We had already done the "Hey Joe" single, "Piss Factory", and we had our little rock/cabaret improvisation thing well under way. Drums were something we had not really thought about, because we were not specifically interested in being a rock-and-roll band . . . we were more a maniac cocktail trio at the time. We were a pretty bizarre band, and Jonathan lent an air of more eccentricity to the proceedings. It was a pretty odd occurrence. There weren't a lot of people around; we were really just getting going. I couldn't get my guitar in tune, and of course playing the Fillmore was a bit special. I guess we must have played some early version of "Land of 1,000 Dances" that was in the works then. I think we were starting to play "Gloria". Jonathan would just kind of bang along.' (In the years since this live appearance Kaye has continued to enjoy Jonathan's work, particularly his ability to 'reinvent a sense of wonder for you' and often goes to see him perform in New York; gigs that are 'a kind of gathering of friends'.)

In March 1975, between the recording and the release of *Chartbusters*, Jonathan returned to New York for another introduction of his new ideas into the rock world – his first live performances in the city since the demise of the Modern Lovers. These would give him a chance to try out some of his new material and his new approach to live performing in a conventional environment. He would bring other musicians with him, too, but not within anything like the formal structure of a regular band – these were friends specially gathered together for these gigs alone.

Jonathan played four nights, the 19th to the 22nd, at the Kitchen, 59 Wooster Street, and among those accompanying him were Andy Paley with his brother Jonathan – and Ernie Brooks. The gigs, all acoustic, featured a mixture of old and new material backed mainly by guitar, bass, percussion and some viola. Occasional a cappella singing added a new dimension, and the performances had a lightness and good humour that did nothing to dilute the emotion of the songs – rather, they complemented it. New material included 'Hi Fred We Still Love You' ('the names have been changed to protect the innocent'), which was a message of reassurance to a friend whose capacity for outrageous and terrible acts may have led to him believe that the outlook for a prolonged friendship was poor, 'New Teller', which would appear on *Chartbusters*, and 'Springtime', which would feature on *Jonathan Richman and the Modern Lovers*.

The band also played 'Here We Are in Dreamland', which had been part of the Modern Lovers' set at the end of their time together. This song continues Jonathan's interest in the world of dreams and its capacity to transcend reality. Towards the end the backing vocals become almost a hypnotic chant, with improvised lyrics laid over, ecstatically bringing new dimensions of love from dream into reality. Of the older songs providing a link with the past, a mesmerizing epic version of 'Roadrunner' pours through the 'lonely industrial high-ways of Massachusetts', pushing images into the air and painting a picture there section by section. The lyrics and vocal performance, overshadowing the musical backing, are what distinguish this per-formance of 'Roadrunner' – and the show as a whole. It is perhaps not surprising that, as a result, after the shows finished Ernie Brooks no longer felt a part of what Jonathan was doing and that these would be their last appearances together for over twenty years. 'It didn't feel quite right, because I wasn't really playing my proper instrument. I felt like . . . someone who's stayed too long at the party, I suppose. I didn't feel that I was adding much. It's funny, I have an acoustic bass now . . .' In the audience for the first night had been Gerard Malanga – an occasion documented by several photographs that he took.

On the 4 July *Beserkley Chartbusters Volume One* was released. Jonathan's four tracks were 'The New Teller', 'Government Center', 'It Will Stand' and a new version of 'Roadrunner' – the first two fea-turing backing by the Rubinoos, the others by Earthquake. The most striking thing about these cuts, given Jonathan's seeming adherence to acoustic instruments and alternative percussion at the time, is their use of electric guitars and bass and full drum kits. Not yet ready to attempt the sonic experiments of *Rock and Roll with the Modern Lovers* (that would take the process of working through a whole album with a new band and much training and rehearsal), Jonathan chooses an amplified power that, allowing for the complete absence of distortion, gives the songs something like the interpretation that the Modern Lovers might have given them (and, in the case of 'Government Center', actually did). There is a definite sense of continuity as a result – particularly so with the presence of 'Roadrunner'. The performances are uniformly sharp and bursting with energy, with no hint of self-indulgence – guitar breaks cram a host of rock-and-roll messages into a few bars – and their conviction is such that there could be no doubts about lack of commitment in Jonathan's new direction. Perhaps the second most striking thing is the lack of new self-penned material – only one song – but this was an album shared with other artists and, although this was a pretty accurate preliminary sketch, a proper depiction of Jonathan's new vision would have to wait for the wider canvas of his first album proper.

The version of 'Roadrunner' does not ignore the freezing loneliness that made its insights possible in the first place, but neither does it dwell on it. It is an uplifting return to the outer-Boston nightscape, emphasizing its excitement and magic against a sparse twin-electric guitar backing – one single-string almost throughout, the other semi-acoustic – and it creates a majestic pop record, finally bringing fulfilment for the anguish that inspired it. This is the version that, on its re-release in 1977, would be a big hit in the UK. (Various singles were initially released from *Beserkley Chartbusters* in the UK through United Artists, who were distributing Beserkley at the time, and 'Roadrunner' was one of them. Despite receiving an ecstatic reception in some quarters, it would have to wait for its moment of glory.)

Even though none of the Modern Lovers' studio material had yet been released, it had already made a significant impact on three people who would soon become highly significant themselves: Glen Matlock, Steve Jones and Paul Cook, shortly to meet John Lydon and to become the Sex Pistols. Nick Kent, the *New Musical Express* journalist, was a regular visitor to Let It Rock, Malcolm McLaren's shop on London's King's Road, and here he got to know the nascent Sex Pistols. He had a tape of the Modern Lovers' first Cale session, and Matlock, Jones and Cook would listen to it and admire its mixture of the 'weird' and the 'simple', as Matlock puts it – for them it was 'a breath of fresh air' at a time when so-called symphonic rock seemed to be permeating all parts of the musical atmosphere. Glen describes Jonathan as 'a very, very major influence' on the Pistols – and John Lydon even went so far in an interview as to name 'Roadrunner' his favourite song. (Incidentally, when Mick Jones was trying to get the Clash together, he would sometimes come down to the Pistols' Denmark Street hangout, in the heart of London's Tin Pan Alley, and here Steve Jones would play drums while Mick Jones and Matlock performed a joint composition about Jackson Pollock that was 'inspired by "Pablo Picasso"')

Through the Beserkley connection, back on the West Coast, Jonathan had now become particularly friendly with the Rubinoos and they started to back him up occasionally in live performances, sometimes singing a cappella while Jonathan played electric guitar, sometimes playing acoustics while he sang. Their bass player, Greg 'Curly' Keranen, would shortly afterwards become a Modern Lover himself.

By now, while mainly playing club dates, the Rubinoos had also been invited to play at Bill Graham's Winterland in San Francisco. This show, also featuring Jefferson Starship, Link Wray and Earthquake, was the first in a new Monday-night series designed to highlight local groups. The Rubinoos were the opening act, and Jonathan, another new challenge presenting itself to him (and one that, in its bizarre nature, rivalled his appearance with the Patti Smith Group), came up on stage and danced while they played a version of the Archies' 'Sugar Sugar'. As Curly says, 'Jonathan was just too clean-cut for the San Francisco hippy mentality', and there was a predictably negative response from around half of the audience. Not so predictable, perhaps, was the positive reaction of the other half, who loved it.

Jonathan would sometimes guest at other Rubinoos gigs, performing one or two songs ('The New Teller' was a favourite), but he made few full-length appearances at this time, preferring to walk around Berkeley, playing guitar and writing songs, continuing the pattern he had established since the break-up of the Modern Lovers of making an organic whole of his life, his outlook and his work.

In June of 1975 Talking Heads had made their live début at the New York punk club CBGB, and on occasions during their formative months 'Pablo Picasso' would be included in their set. David Byrne's early songs would sometimes draw on similar themes to Jonathan's – problems of communication with girls, old-fashioned sexual attitudes, old world/modern world contradictions, 'buildings and food', urban and suburban landscapes – and the band's resolutely unglamorous stage presence (short hair and narrow trousers, casual shirts and T-shirts) was very much in Jonathan's early style. David Robinson caught one of their early appearances and saw plenty of similarities, image-wise, to the Modern Lovers, while Ernie Brooks noted a similar 'naïve' approach to life, and Jerry Harrison (not long afterwards to join them, of course) believes that David Byrne's songs were following on from Jonathan's in their attempt to be concise about subjects that 'really meant something'. There is also a similarity between Talking Heads' early sparse sound and that which Jonathan, as a solo artist, was achieving at a similar time with the *Chartbusters* material. In April 1976 Talking Heads, too, recorded for Beserkley, but this was only a demo, taped in New York. That May they invited Jonathan to play a gig with them at CBGB, but he, having played there a year before with Television, was not keen to repeat the experience, citing as a reason the refusal of bars to let thirteen-year-olds on to their premises, and so turned them down. Shortly after this, their bass player Tina Weymouth and drummer Chris Frantz ran into Ernie Brooks in a New York bar and quizzed him about Jerry Harrison's availability. The band also spoke to Matthew Kaufman and Steve Paul before finally approaching Jerry himself, who at the time was selling computer software in Cambridge, and asking him to join them. Jerry had been considering giving up rock music completely but went to see Talking Heads perform, liked what he heard and, with the band even keener to involve him once they had all played together, the link between the Modern Lovers and Talking Heads was cemented.

By early 1976 the most unlikely recruit possible had joined the band that Jonathan was now putting together, back in Boston, for what would be his first album proper – David Robinson. Now a member of Los Angeles outfit The Pop, David had latterly been on the look-out for an offer that was financially strong enough to enable him to return to Boston. Beserkley tracked him down, informed him that a new version of the Modern Lovers was being put together and offered to pay his air fare back and for an apartment once he arrived.

David spoke to Jonathan, who, unwilling to push his new vision too far too soon, told him that he wanted a proper rock-and-roll drummer for a four-piece, electric-guitar-led band, and David readily accepted the offer. The other members of the new band were Curly Keranen on bass and guitarist Leroy Radcliffe. Curly had grown tired of the Rubinoos after a stint of a couple of years and, after leaving the band, had taken off to Europe, which he had then toured by bicycle. Phoning home from Spain at Christmas-time he was told by his father that Jonathan had been calling from Boston, asking him to be his new (specifically acoustic) bass player. Leroy Radcliffe had previously played in Todd Rundgren's first band and, after a spell out of the music scene, was looking to return. Soon after mentioning this to a disc jockey friend there was a knock on his door one cold February day. Standing there, dressed in shorts and a T-shirt, was Jonathan who had come to check out his skills as a guitarist. Leroy remembers the visit. 'The try-out, if you want to call it that, was not what I was used to. It was a poem more than an interview, and basically it was "Strum along with me, friend, for five minutes." Jonathan was at that time very interested in moments in life, so the moment was a glorious one . . . He presented me with rhythmical challenges, and as he flowed one way, I could flow the other . . . He more or less said I was hired on the spot, although I wasn't sure what I was being hired for!'

After the release of *Chartbusters* Jonathan moved back to Boston, staying in various places, none of which could really be called home, and the new band would be based there, learning new material, rehearsing it and playing a couple of gigs, getting to know each other's playing and developing into a cohesive unit. When the band's preparations were complete, though, and it was finally time for the recording of their first album, they travelled to San Francisco where they would also make another handful of live appearances. This shuttling between Boston and the West Coast would develop into a pattern that would characterize each year of their time together.

*Jonathan Richman and the Modern Lovers* was recorded at the same studio in San Francisco, CBS Folsom Street, as had been used for *Chartbusters* and that would continue to be used for Jonathan's Beserkley material. Despite the rehearsing they had already done, at least a quarter of the songs that appeared on the album were either new to the band at the time of recording or needed to be finalized in the studio. (As always with Jonathan, song-writing was a spontaneous activity, unregimentable, an organic part of life, and the moment needed to cherished. So much so that he would phone Leroy at all hours of the night, trying out melodies and asking for complementary chord sequences.)

Musically *Jonathan Richman and the Modern Lovers* begins very much in the style of fifties and early sixties rock and roll and continues, in the main, the electric sound of the *Chartbusters* material. By its end, however, the sound has begun to acquire new dimensions, and Jonathan's horizons can be seen widening further. On this album we finally get the full opening statement of Jonathan's new outlook and his new way of life, and here love conquers all – there is a lot less of the bleakness that had previously underpinned much of his work. Nevertheless, there is still plenty to conquer: the strangeness of other cultures; a loved one (Gail) who won't admit that she loves him; memories of loneliness, which can still haunt; and man's insensitivity to what he does not understand. Full of joy but serious in intent and constructed with great care, the album works coherently as a whole despite a bold choice of astonishingly diverse material. This ranges from the celebration of the variety that abounds in the USA: 'Rockin' Shopping Center' (a companion piece to 'Government

Center') and a version of Chuck Berry's 'Back in the USA', through the romance of 'Important in Your Life' and 'Hi Dear', the bleakness of 'Lonely Financial Zone' and a trio of 'children's' songs, to the spiritual finale of 'Springtime' and 'Amazing Grace'. For Leroy, there was clear reasoning behind the choice of material: 'He really wanted to make the point to the media and to old fans that he was not going to go down the road of what he thought at the time was influencing young people in the wrong direction. His philosophy was that the old crowd wouldn't understand for a long time, till they maybe got older, what they had actually seen years before – which is probably true. In fact I know it's true.' It was to be the trio of 'children's' songs that would attract the most attention – never happy with traditional examples of the genre (even at kindergarten he had been singled out for refusing to sing along with them) Jonathan had decided to write his own. Public knowledge of him, however, such as it was, consisted largely of memories of the original Modern Lovers, and these songs were – literally, in the case of 'Here Come the Martian Martians' – from a different planet.

The two openers, 'Rockin' Shopping Center' and 'Back in the USA', are very much in the style of the *Chartbusters* material and thus form a bridge to it. 'Rockin' Shopping Center' has two electric rhythm guitars, with clean but driving sounds, and expounds Jonathan's love of the modern world which now encompasses its diversity, finding at least a little fascination everywhere and removing the harshness of his previous criticisms.

'Important in Your Life' pleads for confirmation of the statement that its title makes, and 'New England' takes the geographical positivism of the opening two songs and narrows its focus without doing anywhere else down in the process (it also features an a cappella section and the use of hand claps as percussion – elements to become progressively more important in Jonathan's work).

Although 'Hey There Little Insect' is the only song here that survives from the era of the original Modern Lovers, 'Lonely Financial Zone', full of melancholy beauty, provides a far more authentic echo of it. To an eerie backing of acoustic guitar, bass and light percussion, the song glides with Jonathan into a mysterious other-world, silent but for the buzzing of electric lights. This world is peopled by giant skyscrapers, 'lonely and dark', that have been deserted by their day-time inhabitants and look sadly towards the harbour and the sea front where a life from which they are excluded carries on with the vitality of normality. This is the only song on the album to deal specifically with the loneliness that used to figure so prominently in Jonathan's early years, and even here it is examined indirectly, reflected as it is in the buildings of the financial zone. In this way, it has effectively been transferred (in a similar way to that in which it would be transferred to the 'outsider' figures of the 'children's' songs later in the album) and therefore put at one remove from Jonathan himself – out of harm's way. Jonathan's presence in the song is as an observer, drawing on the magical power of the scene and displacing his own isolation. It is almost as if he is acknowledging the continuing presence of loneliness in his life (as a hugely significant part of his history and of the make-up of his personality it can never be ignored) and reserving the right to continue to be inspired by its creation of magic, while at the same time removing its ability to bring despair. At its end, guitar chords ascend and then fall as if following Jonathan's eyes as they climb one of the skyscrapers and then fall back to earth, bringing the song to a peak of loneliness and beauty and then dissolving it. Leroy recalls the band being with Jonathan 'every breath' on this performance.

'Hi Dear' takes the uncertainty lying underneath 'Important in Your Life' and wills it away, in an echo of some of the songs preserved on the 1974 studio acetate. Here, Jonathan knows that fate has ordained the fruition of his love for Gail at a certain time, and he is waiting far that time to arrive.

'Abominable Snowman in the Market' and 'Here Come the Martian Martians' are the first real sign of Jonathan's love for calypso music, and even here they're given a pretty good rock-and-roll disguise. 'Abominable Snowman' may be partly designed to appeal to children but, like all the 'children's' songs, it's also a plea for tolerance that can be understood by all age groups. Jonathan's own feelings of rejection and other people's lack of understanding are transferred to a figure of legendary isolation and his pathetic attempts to come back in from the cold. Of course the seriousness is offset by the improbability of the setting, and the result is poignant without being sentimental. 'Here Come the Martian Martians' has a similar intent, scenario and form, but the Martians are almost like children – naughty sometimes, anxious to learn, open to abuse. In between these two songs is sandwiched 'Hey There Little Insect', another plea for tolerance and unity, a different balance of power. In all these pieces it's almost as if Jonathan was anxious that their idealism not be seen as po-faced, the humour of the contrasts between the 'characters' and their alien environments providing the necessary foil.

The final two songs (both solo acoustic performances by Jonathan, appropriate to their elemental messages) are 'Springtime' and an adaptation of the traditional 'Amazing Grace' – and they complete the picture the album sets out to paint. Along with what it has already identified as necessary: love for the beauty of what the modern world can produce in a multiplicity of ways, the certainty that romantic love can be won and can transform life, tolerance and community-spirit – a love of humanity – there is a need, too, for love to be linked with the eternal power of the natural world and that of spirituality. 'Springtime' prefigures 'Summer Morning' from *Rock and Roll with the Modern Lovers*, to which it is a companion piece. There is (appropriate to the song's concern with the essence of life) the most primitive of beats here – the occasional sound of Jonathan's knuckles against the soundbox of his solitary guitar. He sings of the beauty of springtime, which is the beauty of life itself as it is reborn, and therefore needs to coexist with love and the beauty of human life. Without this, it can never be fully appreciated and life never fully lived. Jonathan's version of 'Amazing Grace' which concludes the album is a hymn to a personal spirituality that comes from an awareness and acceptance of the universal – the discovery of grace deep within is the key to all that has been espoused in the previous songs. Accompanied again by a single acoustic guitar, he sings of the grace that is inside everyone that just needs to be found and the peace and joy that comes with it, banishing fear, shame, bitterness and isolation and bringing instead peace and a pure self-love. These last two songs, while putting to rest for the time being the solo acoustic performances that Jonathan had been making up to the formation of the new Modern Lovers, also form a bridge between this electric four-piece and the acoustic one that would have developed by the next album.

Predictably, *Jonathan Richman and the Modern Lovers* had rather a bemused reception critically, but to balance the lack of appreciation of those who did not (or did not want to) understand there were more enlightened commentators, such as Giovanni Dadamo who pronounced it a work of genius. Even those who did not like it had problems hiding the fact that they were intrigued.

In England the Sex Pistols had by now torn their way into the national consciousness with music and attitude of a conviction that recalled, in part, the original Modern Lovers, whose work had helped to inspire them. There was a real nihilism to the Pistols, though, that had no place in even Jonathan's most bitter early songs and provided a polar contrast to the album he had just produced. Surprisingly Glen Matlock remembers that *Jonathan Richman and the Modern Lovers* brought a favourable reaction in their London camp: 'Me and Malcolm [McLaren] went to the first Virgin store, at the top of New Oxford Street, by Centrepoint, and we got this record and we took it and we had a little Dansette that we played it on in our Denmark Street hideaway, and we sort of laughed, and Malcolm was going: "Well, it's not really rock and roll, is it?", and I said: "Well, no it ain't, but I quite like it", and he said: "Well, perhaps it's not supposed to be rock and roll." We couldn't work it out, it was such a digression . . . I liked it.'

Unlike *Chartbusters*, which, owing to a lack of funds, had taken a while to appear, *Jonathan Richman and the Modern Lovers* was made available almost immediately. However, although there was a new album to promote, the band did very little live work at this point, soon flying back to Boston.

After only one album, Jonathan's and David's old musical

differences were already emerging again – Jonathan was moving towards an innovative acoustic sound, powerful but low-volume, while David still wanted to be the drummer in a rock band. Jonathan had decided that the new Modern Lovers, as a group, would have to fit in with the tone and subject matter of his new songs and with the way he was now living his life. There would effectively be a collective identity, in much the same the way as there had been in the original band. However, this time the identity would be different and Jonathan's control over it even greater. The band's unity would be streamlined and directed so that it could make a purer expression of a purer philosophy and a purer life – it would almost be an organic extension of Jonathan himself.

The original Modern Lovers had crusaded against certain assumptions and attitudes, and the new version had a similar mission, only this time some of those assumptions and attitudes were different, and this band were going to have to do without the weaponry of loud rock music to help push their message home. They would have to rely instead on their own confidence in their ability to communicate the power of that message – and that would require organization, self-discipline and unanimity. Each band member was now given musical exercises to do: David's involved the removal of his drum kit and the substitution of thigh-slapping and hand-clapping for more conventional percussion. While the rest of the band, seeing Jonathan as way ahead of any one else in his new attitude to volume and dynamics, were happy to follow his vision in this sort of way, David was less happy, feeling instead that there was now a restriction on his freedom to play in a style that was his own. The disenchantment and frustration that David had felt in the original Modern Lovers were returning – and once more he was beginning to feel that he belonged somewhere else.

At this time, too, Jonathan felt that it was important for the band, if they were to be truly integrated into what he was trying to do and properly prepared for the campaign ahead, to retrain not only musically but physically. He began to lead them in a programme of athletic exercises to accompany the more obviously relevant kind.

Curly, a regular yoga practitioner, was happy with this and it fitted in fine with Leroy's lifestyle as well, but for David it was like finding himself in a 'marine boot camp' or a 'religious cult', and he told Jonathan that any fitness routine that he undertook would be of his own volition. While the rest of the band were preparing themselves, ninja-like, for a new kind of rock and roll, David wanted his own development and experimentation to take place within the one that he knew.

Jonathan's lifestyle was more refined, purified and simplified than ever now after his period of reflection, experimentation and relaxation; he knew exactly how he wanted to shape it and he did not permit himself any indulgence – even food and water were limited to what was strictly necessary. His new songs, with their 'purer' subject matter, reflected this new way of life and were expressed sometimes even more concisely than of old and hung on musical structures sometimes even more elemental. However, Jonathan regarded the band's sound, and particularly its volume, as out of step now with these developments and with the application he now wanted to make of what he had learned when playing for children. His vision had to be extended to instrumentation, with its excess being purged. The result would be an extension of the organic whole. For Leroy and Curly this basically entailed a reduction in the volume of their playing – for David, however, Jonathan had other plans. Having already seen the possibilities, with the musical exercises he had set, he started to reduce the size of David's drum kit, gradually eliminating anything that might prevent him from hearing clearly the sound of his own voice. Unlike Leroy and Curly David had to accede to what he saw as a drastic limitation of his capability for self-expression and of his ability to contribute fully to the orchestration of the songs – to him it was almost comparable to a guitarist having the strings removed one by one from his guitar.

Before long, all he had left was a small tom-tom. When this was judged still to be too noisy, he put a towel over it so that it was barely audible. Jonathan then asked him if he could tap on the side of it. He agreed, only to be told that even this was too loud. As far as he was concerned, he had now done all he could. He informed Jonathan that his presence in the band had been reduced to such an extent that he felt he hardly existed any more. It was the summer of 1976. David quit again, and this time it was to be for good. Next stop for him was a punk band called DMZ, and from there he moved on to international success and acclaim for his powerful and intelligent percussion work in the Cars.

As it happened, the owner of the basement in which the band were practising at this time was a drummer known as D. Sharpe, and he asked if he could sit in. He could, and he did, and he got the job – constructing a special drum kit that, with a maximum of controlled energy, would produce authentic sounds at a minimum of volume. D. Sharpe never dragged the beat, despite having to expend so much energy on his kit, and had acute musical awareness (Leroy says he was 'totally sensitive to the split moment before a change'). He also had a drum with a zebra skin on it, played hubcaps – and had a broken arm. In short: he was perfect.

D. Sharpe's approach to percussion was also admirably suited to the kind of public performances Jonathan wanted the new Modern Lovers to give. These, in an extension of the visits the original band had made and his own more recent ones, would be for the disadvantaged and the sick, young and old. These were audiences that were not only deserving but also a real test of the band's ability to project the joy in their songs and, therefore, the perfect preparation for the battle ahead – the attempt to take those songs to rock-and-roll audiences in rock-and-roll venues.

Jonathan would call up hospitals, and the resulting performances there were sometimes given to children in cancer wards, sometimes to those who were deaf. These performances would be all-acoustic and would highlight the 'children's' songs such as 'Here Come the Martian Martians'. The young audiences, who were used to clowns and other traditional entertainers, had never seen anything like this before and, as Leroy says, after a period when they had to be won over, 'all of a sudden would come alive again'. At the old people's homes the band would play for people in their eighties and nineties and would prepare beforehand, learning songs from the turn of the century, such as 'Open the Garden Gate'. The joy that they would bring to and derive from these performances would be a strong confirmation of their collective capability.

With the band now perfectly attuned to low-volume performances Jonathan decided that it was time to do what he had wanted to do for a long time – record a completely acoustic but powerful rock-and-roll album.

In September the band returned to CBS Folsom Street to begin sessions for *Rock and Roll with the Modern Lovers* – in the toilet. Unfortunately the sound here was not exactly what Jonathan had hoped for (the urinals were providing strange reflections), and he decided instead to work in what turned out to be the perfect place: an old echo chamber that had lain unused for the last twenty years. They had already gone to the extent of setting up all their equipment in the men's room, however – and now it had to be moved. When it was finally all set up again in its new location, including remote van, cable and 24-track, everything was perfect. According to Leroy, the key to the success of the operation was microphone placement for balance – they copied the way it used to be done in radio days. (After microphones for each of the four band members had been allocated one channel apiece, the rest of the twenty-four tracks were hardly used.)

A week had been spent making no progress at all, but now the whole album would be completed in less than half that time.

With recording completed, Jonathan Richman and the Modern Lovers headed to New York for what, at the Town Hall on 9 October, would be a showpiece sold-out gig – and a strong test for the new band and its new form of rock and roll.

For live performance the band used a mixture of electric and acoustic instruments, not convinced that a purely acoustic approach, in this kind of venue, would produce an authentic or acceptable sound. What Jonathan wanted instead was something distinctive and personal without being overpowering – he wanted a 'loud' sound at low volume. At this time it was very hard to find an amplifier capable of producing this; the alternative was some creative 'piggybacking', and this was the technique they used.

The set for the Town Hall performance was to include several songs by the original Modern Lovers, material from the new album and its predecessor, one song that has never been recorded, 'Wonderful Girl', and one that would not be recorded until 1985, 'Ancient Long Ago'. Taken as a whole, it was a mixture of the old and the new that would help to smooth the transition between the two.

The compère for the evening told the audience, after they had been entertained by a magician and a juggler, that they would have to entice Jonathan on. They called his name (thus putting themselves on his side before he was even on stage) and he appeared, dressed in a 'University of Santa Clara' T-shirt, shorts, knee-high sports socks and running shoes, his hair now long and curly. Between songs he would drink mineral water. Spirited performances of 'Back in the USA' and then 'Roadrunner' (currying more favour with the audience) were met with enthusiastic applause; 'Rockin' Rockin' Leprechauns', featuring a sax solo from Jonathan (he had recently taken up the instrument again, tenor this time), with astonished delight. Over the course of the evening hecklers, and there were only a few, were dealt with in the style Jonathan had long since perfected: some were ignored, some answered straight and some had their complaints humorously thrown out of court. Requests to turn up the volume were met with a curt 'No'. The first phase of the new Modern Lovers' campaign, conducted with a mixture of high-energy/low-volume rock and roll, technical expertise, discipline and charm, was going down a storm. Encores were a reprised 'Ice Cream Man' and 'Rockin' Rockin' Leprechauns' followed by 'Astral Plane' and 'Wonderful Girl'.

Although the gig was a huge success with an audience by and large willing to suspend its disbelief and follow Jonathan and the band wherever it was taken, some critics still preferred to be outraged. Even Lester Bangs contrived to somehow miss the point, half appreciative, half unable to applaud something that did not fit in with his need for rock music that was loud and depraved. The

*Melody Maker*'s Richard Williams, Velvet Underground fan and ardent espouser of all truly innovative rock music, fell in love and implored 'someone' to bring the Modern Lovers over to Britain 'quick'.

The next year, with the release of *Rock and Roll with the Modern Lovers* and a surprise Top Twenty hit for the re-released 'Roadrunner', someone would.

# 6 AFFECTION

IN 1977 Jonathan would finally achieve the kind of success that the original Modern Lovers glimpsed beyond the horizon, but this time it was going to be on his own terms and he was happy to welcome it.

'Roadrunner' was re-released in Britain. Because Jonathan had gradually received more and more publicity in the eighteen months or so since its first release, the record now attracted a wider circle of admirers, gained radio plays and positive reviews and became a Top Twenty hit, climbing to number twelve. This was the best possible platform for the release that summer of *Rock and Roll with the Modern Lovers* and Jonathan's first ever European tour which would follow on from it.

*Rock and Roll with the Modern Lovers*, if anything, caused more apoplexy, bemusement, declarations of love, devotion and hostility than its predecessor. This time Jonathan had been able to implement the totally acoustic backing that he had been working towards as an organic expression of his new world-view and way of life. This method would reach its peak on the aural landscapes of 'Afternoon' and, particularly, 'Summer Morning'. Once again there were 'children's' songs: 'Rockin' Rockin' Leprechauns' and 'The Wheels on the Bus', but as before these were designed not only to bring a new dimension to children's appreciation and awareness but also to appeal to adults. As with the similar material on *Jonathan Richman and the Modern Lovers* their significance would transcend the traditional limits of the genre. This album would also see the start of Jonathan's documentation of the 'pure' pleasures in his life, as in 'Roller Coaster by the Sea' and 'Ice Cream Man', and the latter would signal the beginning, too, of his interest in childhood as subject matter rather than solely as provider of a genre of songs.

The cover versions (there are four of them here, three of those 'traditional') showed that Jonathan's musical vision and, by extension, his whole outlook now extended world-wide – there is music here from China, Ecuador, Egypt and Jamaica. (As far back as the 1973 *Interview* article Jonathan had indicated a liking for 'any kind of Slavic' music, but *Rock and Roll with the Modern Lovers* contains the first tangible expression on one of his records of a love for songs from non-Western cultures.) Anyone who believes that World Music was 'discovered' in the 1980s would be wise to give 'The Sweeping Wind' and 'South American Folk Song' a listen and prepare to be bewitched.

As a whole, the album ranges, if anything, even wider than *Jonathan Richman and the Modern Lovers*. Part of the reason for this is that love, considered at length on the latter, does not get much of a look-in here. This leaves room for a mixture of mystery, nature, exoticism, essential pleasures and the exploration and recapturing of childhood all of which is capped, as before, by an individual spirituality.

'The Sweeping Wind', which begins the album, has none of the linking factor of the first two songs on *Jonathan Richman and the Modern Lovers*. Here instead is the opening statement of someone whose message, in rock-and-roll terms, is revolutionary. The instrumentation consists of acoustic guitars and bass, triangle, gong and coconut shells – and it is an instrumental Chinese folk tune. There is no electric power here, there are no drums and no words, and there is no apparent connection with the Anglo-American rock-and-roll tradition within which the track would be presumed to be working.

There is, however, a beauty, a simplicity and an awareness of the power of dynamics, together with an ability to harness sensitivity and joy. The combination brings a strength and a passion that refuses to accept the existence of 'rules' and creates a performance that has everything that is also contained by the best rock and roll. You can hear the players breathing, and you can hear their fingers moving up and down the guitar strings – there is a real sense of their presence, the kind rarely conveyed by conventional studio-refined productions.

After 'shock of the new' of 'The Sweeping Wind', 'Ice Cream Man' brings back a little familiarity. It has a lyric, one to which every Anglo-American can easily relate, and gone are the gong and coconut shells, replaced by a tambourine – not exactly a drum kit but recognizably rock and roll. It lacks a chorus as such, but the repetition of 'Ice Cream Man' fulfils the function, and there is a guitar solo that may be acoustic but rocks just the same. The chimes of the ice cream van create an almost Pavlovian excitement and happiness in Jonathan – and to encapsulate them in song is to create, in a process of musical alchemy, feelings of joy that are every bit as real. Here Jonathan brings his childhood back into the present in a process that would be increasingly a part of the purification and enhancement of his life and would assume a similarly important place in his work.

'Rockin' Rockin' Leprechauns' is another 'alien' song, like the ones of the previous album. Musically it's a similar rock-and-roll/calypso fusion, but lyrically there is another variation as the leprechauns reclaim their twilight world to exercise their new-found love of innocent pleasures.

'Summer Morning' is the album's peak in terms of fulfilment of the possibilities of an all-acoustic approach. The slow unwinding of a summer's day as the natural world comes to life emerges through a yawning, bowed bass, splashes of acoustic guitar, percussive creaks and shuffles, shakes and shimmers and then a metronomic, tapping cymbal and a birdlike fluttering. Sometimes you can hear Jonathan gasp in the instrumental passages and in the pauses before he sings. 'Summer Morning' is the first example of Jonathan sharing a song-writing credit – the next would not come for many years – and Leroy, his co-writer, explains how the arrangement worked: 'Basically, all the chord changes were mine; he brought the emotion, almost like a one-man play, in the song. He sang a melody and I improvised the structures behind it. I devised it with him over the period of a day or two.'

'Afternoon' is a companion piece to 'Summer Morning'. The two-chord structure alternates between reflection and an up-tempo reggae beat and the song celebrates the spirit of nature: unifying but mysterious, with plants and trees communicating to people and a pale moon visible at the same time as the sun.

The original Modern Lovers' 'Fly into the Mystery' finally makes an appearance on album here – pretty much unaltered but with the emphasis more on 'life's mystery' – and the acoustic treatment gives it room to breathe and to flow.

'South American Folk Song' – Jonathan would later trace it to Ecuador – starts what, in its original vinyl form, was the album's second side, mirroring the first side's Chinese folk song, 'The Sweeping Wind'. There is a similar application of rock-and-roll dynamics and changes of pace here, with most of the rhythm duties undertaken by acoustic guitar, leaving D. Sharpe to come up with a little suitably Latin percussion together with various other effects that defy description. The result is a magical translation of South America up to the USA.

'Roller Coaster by the Sea' is like an acoustic Ramones song, with a similar regard for simple pleasures set to an unrelenting beat and a great pop tune. The pleasure is entirely pure, and it is that purity that allows it to cleanse the feeling of sadness that preceded it.

Together with its predecessor, 'Dodge Veg-O-Matic' shows the rock-and-roll power that can be created by using acoustic instruments alone. D. Sharpe's low-volume but high-power drum kit is shown at its best here, and the rhythm-guitar-playing makes up in energy anything it might have lost in the absence of electricity. A tale of love between man and automobile, 'Dodge Veg-O-Matic' turns the usual lust for speed, sleekness and shiny metal on its head.

'Egyptian Reggae' is a wonderful culture clash, a variation of the old music-hall 'Sand Dance' set to a reggae beat and beautifully orchestrated. At the end of this year and the beginning of the next it would be a big hit all over Europe and number six in the charts in Britain.

This is followed by a more traditional kind of song, a version of Desmond Dekker's 'Coomyah'. Jonathan's interest in reggae was a logical extension of the one he had already shown in calypso and paralleled the interest being shown at the time by the more aware British punk bands, many of whom were also citing the original Modern Lovers as an influence.

The definition 'children's song' may have been too restrictive for the likes of 'Here Come the Martian Martians' and 'Abominable Snowman in the Market', but it certainly fits 'The Wheels on the Bus', a traditional, if rather banal, playground favourite. There is an extra passenger on this bus, however, bringing mystery and a little fear and livening things up no end – he is a monster and, by the song's end, the adults, anxious to restore the order apparent throughout the original version of the song and familiar from their own youth, have got rid of him and his otherworldly indiscipline. Musically, too, there is added life – this is a real rock-and-roll song now, with a stronger rhythmic core, particularly on the added chorus, and a guitar break of compressed power.

There may be leprechauns and monsters in Jonathan's terrestrial world, but above it there are angels – he 'can feel it' and believes it 'now more every day'. 'Angels Watching Over Me' is sung a cappella with finger-clicking and hand-clapping support – grateful, hopeful and joyful. Jonathan propels the words along almost as if he is willing them into life (as he had earlier willed the reciprocation of his love) – his belief necessary to their truth.

Before the band set off for their first foreign tour they had to find a new bass player, as Curly was temporarily returning to college. Asa Brebner worked in a health food shop in Cambridge, Massachusetts, and Jonathan, who loved health food, was a regular visitor there – good eating, in fact, had long been both a pleasure and an important part of his lifestyle. Now it was also to lead him directly to his new bass player. During their conversations Asa revealed that he was a guitarist and, although not experienced on the four-string variety, was happy to practise. Once more, Jonathan had stumbled across a new recruit at exactly the right time.

Two months later the band left for Europe. On Jonathan's arrival in England (unrecognizable from the figure with long curly hair on the sleeve of *Rock and Roll with the Modern Lovers* – he now had very short, recently cut hair, together with a pencil-thin moustache that had been around rather longer) he was driven to Beserkley's HQ in Kingston, just outside London. Once there, to the subsequent fascination of the music press who were not really used to this kind of behaviour from rock-and-roll stars, he insisted on jogging the nine miles to his hotel.

For this first English tour, just four dates were arranged: Manchester, Birmingham and two nights at London's Hammersmith Odeon. The summer of 1977 was the peak of punk rock in Britain and, for the London gigs, a cross-section of its hierarchy was in attendance, including members of the Sex Pistols and the Clash, together with every kind of music business/press representation. Glen Matlock recalls visiting the Odeon. 'That was one of the most interesting gigs I've ever been to in my life, at the beginning anyway, because we went in there – Joe Strummer, Mick Jones, there was about eight of us – and there was a massive big stage and there's a little drum kit, the bass player and guitarist with tiny little amps and they set up right in the middle of the stage. We came in and everybody's going: "Shhh! You're making too much noise!"; but it was great, it was riveting because everybody was giving him all of their attention.'

At Manchester's Free Trade Hall the audience included Pete Shelley of the Buzzcocks, probably the punk band most in tune with Jonathan's sensibility. Some of the first copies of *Beserkley Chartbusters Volume One* and *The Modern Lovers* to make it into England were in the Buzzcocks' record collections, and the Jonathan was an acknowledged influence, as Pete remembers: '*The Modern Lovers*, even if you play it now, it could be a new band. I'm sure at soundchecks and rehearsals we used to do "Roadrunner", and on occasions I played "Pablo Picasso" – not to an audience, though! I've always had a soft spot for Jonathan. Early on we got the *Jonathan Richman and the Modern Lovers* album and we used to play that. I'm sure that had a lot more influence than people normally give it.'

At the English shows, following the pattern in the USA, a tiny but vocal minority did not like what they saw and heard, and Jonathan would counter their interruptions in time-honoured fashion, but most of the people who were not already determined to hate the band were, by the end, delighted and enchanted, and there would be encore after encore.

This second stage in Jonathan's new campaign had looked like being the hardest – Leroy recalls being warned beforehand about the possible negative reaction of audiences. 'Can you imagine going in front of a bunch of punks and rockers and playing "Ice Cream Man" and have them not both join forces and come for the stage and kill you? It was pretty ballsy.' By now, however, after lengthy preparation, both mental and physical, rehearsals, and live performances in venues that had already ranged from hospitals and old people's homes to New York Town Hall, the band considered themselves able to stand up to pretty much anything – and so it proved.

One of the gigs on the German leg of this European tour took place in a large amphitheatre in Hamburg. Half a song into the set here, as Asa recalls, Jonathan called a halt and sat down on the side of the stage. Here he took off his shoes and socks and explained, as far as this was possible across the language barrier, that he was trying to remove a splinter. The audience, already uncertain what to make of the band, started shouting abuse. Jonathan responded by saying that they could have their money back if that was what they wanted – and Asa wondered how long it would be before missiles started to rain on the stage. Before things got that bad Jonathan got back on to his feet and the band struck up again. The atmosphere eased slightly. Later on, however, having refused to play 'Pablo Picasso', the band were booed by a section of the audience and other people started screaming at them, believing that they had been cheated. Somehow

Jonathan managed to restore a calm, which then became total silence – and the band played 'Hospital'. There was a standing ovation, with some of the audience crying. Leroy recalls it as a moment that was 'almost historical'.

Meanwhile, at Hammersmith, the band played their usual mixture of material, including 'Astral Plane', 'Roadrunner' and 'She Cracked'. They also played a version of 'Wimoweh' that was made up on the spot, completely unrehearsed, in response to an audience request. There was, as has always been the case with Jonathan's live performances, no such thing as an official set-list. These, for Jonathan, impose an order that could be inappropriate, are incompatible with the natural development of an evening's individual mood and restrict one of the factors most cherished by Jonathan in a performance – the unpredictable.

After the Sunday night gig, the final one of the tour, about eighteen people gathered around a table at Newton's in London's King's Road to celebrate. There was a lot of food, and not all of it was eaten. Jonathan, so opposed to profligacy in all aspects of life, was not happy about the waste, especially as it had been created, partly at least, in his name. He got everyone to pass their plates to him and finished off what was left.

While in England Jonathan decided that he would go against his natural instincts and agree to do some press interviews – something he had been wary of since having previous remarks misquoted and taken out of context. Although, for the most part, he was to get a sympathetic hearing and accurate transcriptions this time, it was not something he would ever do again to this extent. In these 1977 interviews Jonathan was happy to talk about the past, up to a point, and showed an awareness of the punk movement, to whom the original Modern Lovers had been such an inspiration.

While 'Egyptian Reggae' was in the charts in Britain the band appeared on television, along with the Buzzcocks, on *Top of the Pops*. The programme's policy of asking performers to mime to their hit singles was not one that appealed to Jonathan, whose guitar-playing on this occasion showed little sign of having created the sounds emerging from millions of television sets. Pete Shelley remembers encountering him at the *Top of the Pops* studios, a meeting that did not really involve anything as formal as a conversation. 'He seemed quite absorbed in his own world. I was going down some stairs, and he was, like, hopping up them! I just stopped till he hopped to the top and then he sort of sheepishly looked at me when he realized I'd been watching him hopping up the stairs!'

In October 1977 Jonathan and the band were back in Boston. On the 29th they played New York again, this time at the university. The set was largely familiar but also took in five cover versions, a song never to be recorded ('I Am Now a Little Boy Once More') and an instrumental jam featuring a truly terrible trombone solo from Jonathan – although no less appealing because of it. Highlights were a lean, dub-like version of 'Afternoon', a rare, slowed-down 'Sweeping Wind' and a poignant 'Hospital', which had an introduction linking it to events that occurred near the university hall where the gig took place. 'Roadrunner' took a drive via Route 62 from the north shore down to the south shore and further down, where Route 3 meets route 128, down to Cohasset where, on a fall night at forty degrees, the air was 'misting 'cause we're near the ocean'. A triumphant 'The Morning of Our Lives' (a kind of updating of 'A Plea for Tenderness') was the climax to the set – one that had built on the success of the year before.

By now Jonathan had firmly established his new direction, together with the kind of audience that would appreciate it. He had achieved what he had aimed for and the band's US mission was complete – after one more visit to Europe the same would apply there, too. The same time next year they would no longer exist.

Jonathan was at this point close to succeeding in his campaign to woo Gail, who, to complicate matters, now had a young son, Jason. Despite the moral dilemma Jonathan was firm in his belief that a decision to leave her husband to come and live with him must be the right one. His new material now would lean strongly towards this hoped-for reunion and, when it was finally achieved, would deal substantially with it.

Jonathan had formed the original Modern Lovers for two main reasons: because he was lonely and because he felt that he had a cause that could be pursued better with the support of a band. With the second version of the Modern Lovers there was certainly a cause once again, but, once that cause had been successfully pursued and once the presence of Gail had removed the loneliness that still remained, there was no real future for them. They would soon find themselves, like their namesakes, with their volume being turned down and down until, finally, there was no volume at all.

At the end of 1979 Beserkley, capitalizing on the success of the first European tour, released *Modern Lovers Live*, which had been recorded at the Hammersmith Odeon. The album included several songs that had not previously been released. Of these, 'I'm a Little Dinosaur' loses a lot of its impact without the listener being able to see Jonathan, on all fours, crawling behind the drum kit as the band 'plead' for him to return. It's almost as if he is acting out here, in the guise of another 'outcast' species, the way he has come in from the cold of his youthful loneliness, with the tolerance and love asked for in the other 'alien' songs actually being given. If ever a live album could have done with an accompanying video, this, in the days before such things were common, was it. The between-songs patter, however, featuring Jonathan indulging in plenty of banter with the audience, was wonderful enough to create a good impression of what it was like actually to be there.

In January 1978 'The Morning of Our Lives' was released as a single in Britain, soon becoming a third successive Top Thirty hit. However, although it looked as if the new year was beginning with Jonathan's career at a commercial peak, none of his remaining Beserkley singles would make a mark and his next tour, much larger in scale, would be his last with the band. Once again Jonathan would apparently turn his back on success.

'The Morning of Our Lives' was not as successful as Jonathan's previous two singles, with a highest placing of only twenty-eight, but it helped keep him in the public eye in the period leading up to his second European tour in early spring.

In May Jonathan Richman and the Modern Lovers returned to the UK, this time for an extensive eighteen-date tour. By now, confusingly, Jonathan had rejected his 'Clark Gable' look in favour of something approaching his earlier long-haired but clean-cut incarnation. His appearance had also changed somewhat in another way – in the battle to balance two of his major interests, eating and exercising, the former was currently, if temporarily, holding sway. The music, though, had stayed much the same, apart from the addition of a few songs, such as 'Affection' and 'Abdul and Cleopatra' that would later appear on *Back in Your Life*. Sets were becoming longer now – the Leeds Polytechnic gig clocked in at over two hours, and the larger audiences, now knowing what to expect, sang along and called out requests.

While in the UK this time, Jonathan gave a long interview to Nick Kent for the *New Musical Express*. On the way to the interview at Beserkley's Kingston headquarters Kent shared a car with Jonathan, Leroy, Asa and publicist Eugene Manzi. The initial stages of the journey, with Jonathan seemingly not in the best of moods and the atmosphere 'dour', did not augur well, but suddenly he started singing, unaccompanied apart from his own beating of time on the dashboard, 'line following line, verse following verse . . . sentiment after sentiment . . . for . . . a whole fifteen minutes', according to Kent. Apart from the odd phrase, the lyrics were entirely improvised, and Kent, stunned and intrigued, found his initial foreboding magically dispelled. Two hours of interview saw Jonathan reliving his first impressions of the Velvet Underground, describing his earliest songs, the Cale demos and the split with the original Modern Lovers – even treating Kent to a spontaneous rendition of 'Affection'. During the interview Kent brought up the subject of punk rock and the Sex Pistols in particular, citing Jonathan's current music as a polar opposite and concluding that, although Jonathan's stance may have seemed cute, it was actually 'every bit as relevant as . . . and much braver' than 'the tracts of the nihilism brigade'. Kent, initially sceptical, was charmed, and Jonathan had another influential admirer – this time someone who, as an avowed espouser of the cause of the 'punk' lineage, gave his blessing to Jonathan's new direction. When asked what his personal ambition was, Jonathan replied that it was to have a wife and kids – an ambition that was soon to be realized.

Kent's interview referred to the new Jonathan Richman and the Modern Lovers album (then to have been called *Modern Love Songs*), rough mixes of which had already been made. On its eventual and re-titled appearance, though, the album would not exclusively feature the Leroy/Asa/D. Sharpe band – by the end of the European tour they were no longer a unit.

Things came to a head at a gig in Liverpool, as Leroy remembers. 'It actually ended at a soundcheck, where I personally could not play any lower . . . I started to feel: He's being unreasonable. He was getting feistier and feistier, and I think he needed to break out. I'm the one who actually put it in his heart, I said: "What we feel right now is you're not letting us perform, you're not happy and we're not happy, either." I didn't expect him to react so quickly, it was a little bit shocking to me, after all we'd been through . . . I still feel good about what we accomplished.'

By this time, D. Sharpe had already decided to follow his first love, jazz, by joining Carla Bley's band (he would also later sit in on drums for John Lurie's Lounge Lizards), and this, together with Leroy's willingness to go along with the decision, decided Jonathan that the time was right to play solo again. Once more he had lowered and lowered the band's volume until it disappeared altogether.

Asa Brebner would return to play with Jonathan in the mid-eighties, but Leroy, after a stint with Asa backing Robin Lane in her band the Chartbusters, was to give up full-time music.

The songs he played while in the Modern Lovers are 'still a part' of him, however, and, having once had to turn down an invitation from Jonathan to take part in a small tour because he was unavailable, he would be very happy to accept a similar opportunity in the future if it were to arise.

The band's swan song, *Back in Your Life* – with Jonathan, displaying an ongoing interest in his original choice of career, contributing a moonlight landscape to the sleeve – was not to be released until the year after it was recorded. By this time the tracks previously recorded for it in California – predominantly electric in instrumentation – had been supplemented by material from an acoustic session with Andy Paley and other friends of Jonathan's on Long Island.

The album, despite the use of two completely different sessions with strikingly different instrumentation, is very much a coherent whole. Love is a major theme again, after the 'Rock and Roll' of the previous studio album – in fact it is dealt with in one form or another in every single song. The title says it all: this is an album about the reuniting of Jonathan and Gail (the original title of *Modern Love Songs* would, with this reunion effected, not have been specific enough). The only songs not to come under the umbrella of romantic love are the two 'children's' songs and 'Affection', and they ask for a more general form of love, the kind that can be supportive of true romance.

By now Jonathan had broken the ground that he had wanted to, firmly establishing his new direction and the mixture of old fans and new who would want to follow his career. This album, therefore, has no need to be revolutionary and has Jonathan settling into his new environment.

'Affection' is a song that would be a regular part of Jonathan's live shows for several years, during which time it would be added to and improvised on substantially (Asa recalls the band in their performances of it trying to get Jonathan to 'rock it out a little more', whereas he preferred to use it as a way of talking directly to the audience). This is Jonathan's account of the reasons for the 'change' in his musical style, and it is also a personal manifesto and a plea for people to assess their priorities in favour of emotion rather than materialism. Towards the end of the album a version appears of an old American Civil War piece, 'Emaline', a frozen episode from the past now unfrozen, a love affair preserved from many years ago and relived in song. In terms of mood it paves the way for the final song, 'I Hear You Calling Me', which again closes an album on a spiritual note. Its subject is love after death, eternal love, an apt projection of what has been the abiding concern of the album: the relationship that Jonathan sees developing between Gail and himself.

By the summer of 1979, when *Back in Your Life* finally came out, there was of course no band to promote it. Despite some appreciative reviews the commercial momentum of 1977–8 had been lost, and it would not be until 1983, despite regular recording sessions, that Jonathan's next album would be released.

**1** Jonathan on stage with the Modern Lovers,
*c.* 1971

*photographer unknown*

**2, 4** Jonathan on stage at the Modern Lovers'
second gig, Cambridge YMCA, USA, 1971

*photographer unknown*

**3** Jonathan with David Robinson at the
Cambridge YMCA, 1971

*photographer unknown*

5

5  The Modern Lovers in Boston, April 1971

*Thomas Consilvio*

6  Jonathan at a Modern Lovers' gig in a
US church hall, *c.* 1971

*Thomas Consilvio*

6

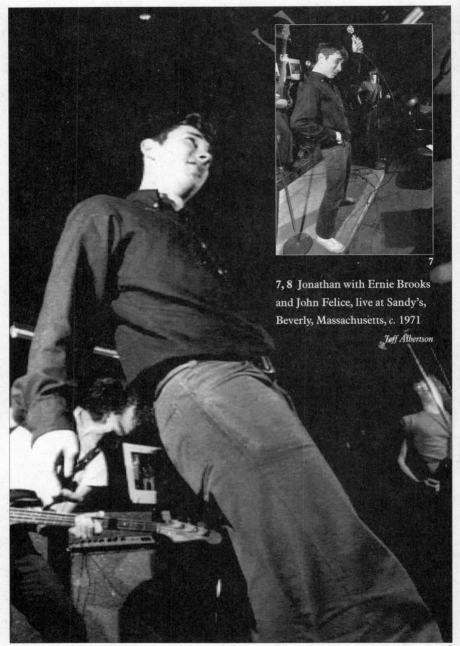

**7, 8** Jonathan with Ernie Brooks
and John Felice, live at Sandy's,
Beverly, Massachusetts, *c.* 1971

*Jeff Albertson*

7

**9, 10, 11, 12** Jonathan and Ernie at Sandy's

*Jeff Albertson*

13

14

The Modern Lovers playing at Boston's
Stone Phoenix, *c.*1971

*photographer unknown*

**13** David Robinson

**14** Ernie Brooks

**15** Jerry Harrison

**16, 17, 18** Jonathan

15

16

17

18

**19** The Modern Lovers, Cambridge Common, Massachusetts, *c.*1972

*Kevin J. Cummisky*

**20** Promotional shot of the Modern Lovers, 1973

*Richard P. Rogers*

**21** Jonathan and the Modern Lovers (from left: D. Sharpe, Leroy Radcliffe, Asa Brebner) in the dressing-room of the Hammersmith Odeon, London, September 1977

*photographer unknown*

**22** Beth Harrington (left) and Ellie Marshall, the Rockin' Robins, who sang with Jonathan in the 1980s

*Catherine McDermott*

23 Jonathan playing to the gallery at the Mean
Fiddler, London, June 1998

*Tim Mitchell*

24 Jonathan playing for friends, Washington, DC,
1992

*Tony Jonaitis*

25 Jonathan making an in-store appearance in
Cambridge, Massachusetts, 1992

*Tony Jonaitis*

26 The end of a gig, Cambridge, England,
June 1992

*Rob Stickells*

27 The day after the 1992 Cambridge gig

*Rob Stickells*

25

26

27

28

**28** Jonathan with the Velvet Underground's Sterling Morrison, Austin, Texas, 1985

*Martha Morrison*

# 7 SOMEBODY TO HOLD ME

WHILE travelling by train to New York from Boston in the spring of 1979, accompanied only by his guitar and his knapsack, Jonathan met a fellow passenger, Robin Radin, who recorded the experience in a diary and later published the account in *New York Rocker*. Jonathan was wearing track shoes, sweatshirt and flared jeans, and his guitar was decorated with red and green hearts, as on the sleeve of *Back in Your Life*.

Robin offered Jonathan some fruit and fell asleep to the rhythm of the train, only to wake shortly afterwards to the sound of singing. The song was 'Hi Dear', and Jonathan was performing it for an appreciative audience of passengers, young and old, who had turned around in their seats to watch him. Jonathan stopped to eat an apple and told Robin about his projected next album, to be solo and acoustic, before taking up his guitar again to play some of the songs he wanted to appear on it. Pausing once more to talk of his love for his guitar ('We've gone through lots together'), he then went on to play an hour's worth of older songs that included 'Roadrunner' and 'Abominable Snowman in the Market'. His audience loved it; even the conductor nodded his head in approval, and Jonathan blushed as he acknowledged their applause. Then the sky began to darken, the audience became passengers again and Jonathan took out a book. Another gig was over.

The album Jonathan was talking about never appeared – it was one of many projects upon which he would embark over the next few years that would not make it on to vinyl. Many of these recordings were made with Andy Paley and a variety of backing musicians – ranging from no one to a whole orchestra – in a variety of environments: one session was conducted at Jonathan's apartment, one with a portable recorder in nearby woods, others by the Charles River and in an eight-track studio. All of these were intended to become records and, although none actually did, many of the songs would appear, re-formed, sooner or later on Jonathan's albums.

Having firmly established his new approach with the second incarnation of the Modern Lovers, and, with their disbandment, campaign successfully completed, having effectively announced a further stage in his development, Jonathan could finally consign the old songs to their era and leave them there – although he would reserve the right to relive them occasionally, when appropriate. His parallel campaign, to win Gail, was on the verge of fruition, too, and the loving relationship that he had always craved was within his grasp. With his own personal happiness growing, and much of what had been a burden to him removed, Jonathan was now freer than ever to pursue his new vision and to implant it into his songs and their performance. None of this, however, should suggest that his past would be forgotten – it would always be a part of him but could now be viewed with objectivity as well as emotion.

On the sessions recorded at his apartment in Cambridge in the summer of 1979 Jonathan was preparing for an album that was to be called *Jonathan Richman Sings*. (By 1983, on the album's eventual appearance, only a couple of the songs from these original sessions would survive, re-recorded, a full and full-time band would be present – creating a very different sound and embodying a very different approach – and the album's title would have shortened to *Jonathan Sings!*) There is plenty of chat between the songs and there are also false starts, abrupt curtailments (including a version of 'Land of 1,000 Dances') and joke items. Although plenty of work was done, it seems to have been at least as important for everyone to enjoy themselves. At this time he was very much a solo act when playing live, but recording was different, and here Jonathan's acoustic guitar is accompanied by two female backing singers and a second guitar, acoustic and electric, of Leroy Radcliffe, happy to undertake some more recording with Jonathan. One of the backing singers is Ellie Marshall, whom he had first met on returning from the European tour of 1978. She would record with him from 1979 until 1986 and, as well as continuing to be a personal friend, has often opened shows for him since then.

Ellie was fifteen when she met Jonathan and used to sing occasionally with her brothers' band, the Marshalls, in Scituate just outside Boston. Andy Paley was a friend and would bring different people along to see them play. Sometimes he would bring Jonathan – and sometimes Jonathan would get up and sing 'Roadrunner' or 'Little Sister'. Ellie's sister Jeannie had written a poem called 'My Modern Lover' (both sisters were fans of the album *The Modern Lovers*), and Ellie came up with some music for it, recording it a year later on a four-track, with Andy Paley producing.

By this time Ellie would see Jonathan around occasionally; he would greet her with 'Hey, Marshall!' and remember her as the girl who sang 'It's My Party' with her brothers' band. Andy played Jonathan Ellie's demo, and Jonathan phoned her up soon afterwards to say that he loved it, had played it eight times in a row and that it had made him cry every time and feel beautiful and young. This was the first of many phone calls from Jonathan to Ellie, calls that would eventually lead to him coming over and singing, then to the two of them singing together and finally to the recording of a series of demos for what would eventually become *Jonathan Sings!*

Recorded during the session at Jonathan's apartment was a version of 'Bundle of Joy', a song that was originally to have appeared on *Back in Your Life* – its message one of gratitude to the angels that they have sent him someone to reciprocate his love perfectly. There is also a version of 'I Love Her Little Body'. Almost every part of the body features in the lyric, and it is as if it is recreated there, part by part, and laid out within the structure of the song. A between-songs meander around the subject of coyotes in Central Park takes a bizarre direction: 'This is going to be a big hit with coyotes and jackals. Twenty-five years from now, when they excavate all these jackals' dens . . . [they'll] find all these Jonathan Richman records all scratched up because they've been played all the time.' As well as his own material Jonathan plays several covers here, with a mixture of appropriate subjects from romance and longing to conviction and holding on to the vision of youth: 'This Little Light of Mine', 'Ruby', 'Crazy Little Mama', 'Sugar and Spice', 'Young at Heart' and 'Wedding Bells'.

There are several songs on the eight-track demos, recorded at Perfect Crime studios at the end of the summer, that have never been released in any form. One of these is 'When My Mother Met Your Mother on the Checkout Line', which Jonathan had already been performing live. Doo-wop in flavour and accompanied by acoustic guitar, bass, hand claps and backing vocals, it is an unlikely testament to the power and pleasure of gossip between two women. Encompassing everything from disease to divorce, the particular, protracted session discussed in the song stretches on from 'gossip breakthrough' to 'gossip heaven' – at which point the two practitioners are 'like little girls again', completely liberated from the restrictions of politeness and completely at ease with one another. 'That's Rock and Roll' is another celebration of the power of music and dancing, and a companion piece, 'Brand New Dance', is probably the sexiest thing Jonathan has ever recorded. Set to a slinky reggae beat, sliding along on bass, drums and rhythm guitar and with teasing female backing vocals ('Stop! Mr Richman, I . . . '), it skanks along in a rocksteady groove, slowly punching out its dance-floor instructions.

There is also the very special, and completely unaccompanied, 'That Five-Year-Old Feeling'. Like 'Ice Cream Man' before it, in this song Jonathan aims to recapture the feeling of childhood while he is singing about it. Here, however, as images and smells are summoned back (a lavender house and a white Buick car, playground dirt, the 'wet and wild' weeds), the process occurs through a real effort of will and takes the song on to a different scale of intensity – Jonathan reactivates the memories of a childhood consciousness and relives what it is like to be a five-year-old. This is one of the most potent and poignant moments in Jonathan's whole musical life, and the emotion nearly breaks his voice. The fact that it has never been made publicly available is a tragedy.

'That Five-Year-Old Feeling' is one of what would prove to be a series of songs about childhood in which Jonathan tries to recapture the purity of feelings and the excitement felt as a child and to implant them into adulthood. For Jonathan, children are seldom given the combination of self-determination and adult respect that would allow them to enjoy their experiences fully – in this way, however, later on in life, the magic can be recreated in just such an environment.

Although none of Jonathan's recorded work from the period 1979–81 was to see the light of day he continued to make recordings and to enjoy doing so. He also continued to make low-key solo public performances in the USA and Europe in the style of his appearances after the demise of the original Modern Lovers – despite rumours that he had retired.

Without a band once again, Jonathan could repeat the process of consolidation, renewal and departure of that earlier period. This time, though, with the battle to establish his new approach publicly already won, and his personal happiness on a new level, the process would not culminate in an organized 'campaign', as in 1976–8, but it would result in a new band.

Even now he was already considering the formation of his next line-up of Modern Lovers, one that would not have to fight the battles of its predecessors. Ellie Marshall would be a member and so would Curly Keranen who, after three years of studying statistics, began a year of 'hanging around' with Jonathan.

A solo show at Washington's Cellar Door in October featured Jonathan on electric guitar and saxophone solos, occasional approximation of a drumbeat courtesy of the kicking of his cowboy boots against the stage and, where they could be fitted in, his own backing vocals.

Alone again on a stage Jonathan was now able to express himself completely, free from the added complications and compromise that other people brought to his songs but with what was by now a refined theatricality unmistakable for artifice. Brecht would have been envious – the songs mixed didacticism with entertainment; they would be interrupted without warning by monologues, a cappella sections and instrumental passages – and the audience's attention would never be anything other than fully engaged. Having returned to rock-and-roll venues with the second incarnation of the Modern Lovers and firmly laid down the way he would perform in them and the kind of material he would use, Jonathan, as a solo act, would now make more frequent and regular club appearances – but would certainly not restrict himself to them.

By November Jonathan had bought his first car and was about to leave Boston and move to Maine, and it was from here that Jonathan phoned Andy Paley with an idea for his next project: he wanted to record with an orchestra.

Taking on such a huge musical backing might be considered a strange step for Jonathan, so keen on presenting his songs as directly and simply as possible – particularly when he had only recently decided that three musicians, playing at low volume, were too intrusive – but there is a logic to it. In the studio Jonathan would have complete control of the sound and there would be no chance of being drowned out. The musicians playing with him would be hired for a specific project, with no commitment to touring or further albums – this would be a one-off. Also Jonathan's increasingly relaxed outlook and sense of freedom allowed him to range ever wider – and this was a project that would provide a considerable contrast to the minimal accompaniment to many of the songs on *Back in Your Life*. The shock value of that contrast would guarantee that people sat up and took notice. And finally, an orchestra would provide a suitably romantic backdrop to the love songs he wanted to sing for Gail.

As one of the Paley Brothers, and while recording with the Ramones, Andy Paley had been working with Phil Spector; he decided to give him a call. If Jonathan was going to work with an orchestra there could be no better collaborator than the man who had created the 'wall of sound'. Spector, purely as a favour, got together a full orchestra and horn section for the recordings. Jonathan then started to arrange some of the material he wanted to use – aided by the late Ray Pullman ('one of the all-time great bass players', in Andy's words), who would also play on the session.

Recording took place, with the assistance of Spector's staff, at Gold Star, the studio where the original Modern Lovers had attempted for the final time to make a proper album. Jonathan's vocals were recorded at the same time as the backing track, so the horns and orchestra leaked through his microphone; Matthew Kaufman describes the resulting mix as 'just magic'. A wide variety of material was recorded, including versions of Sam Cooke's 'Cupid' and a Bing Crosby song 'Let's Take the Long Way Home'. However, as with the rest of the material from this period in Jonathan's career, none of it would be released commercially. Jonathan played the completed tape, which was scheduled to appear as his next album, for Curly Keranen one day and asked his opinion. Curly thought that the contrast between his voice and the 'wall of sound' was too great, that they were incompatible. Jonathan listened to the tape again, agreed and told Matthew Kaufman that he did not want the album released.

Curly identified one track, however, that in his opinion stood out from the rest: the interpretation of 'Let's Take the Long Way Home'. Framed by spoken introduction and conclusion this features, as well as the orchestra, harp, drums and bass. The lyrics, with their references to magic, dreams, the moon and the stars, are sung with relish. However, although there is real beauty here, it is not, finally, the kind of setting that suits Jonathan's vocal style best. A version of 'Up in the Sky Sometime' (a different one would later appear on the *Rockin' and Romance* album) was also recorded; this makes a companion piece for 'Let's Take the Long Way Home' – another night-time trip through the stars with a similarly ethereal feel.

In early 1980 Jonathan had played his first New York concert for two years at Irving Plaza. A ninety-minute set of twenty-two songs had included a mixture of old material (including an a cappella fourth encore of 'Angels Watching Over Me'), new songs and several cover versions. Jonathan had played a cheap Japanese electric guitar bought earlier that day, received gifts from the audience (including flowers, little plastic dinosaurs and a rubber Martian) and had sat on the stage afterwards exchanging words, handshakes and hugs with the audience.

On 23 May Jonathan made a return visit to New York, playing this time at Club 57. This was a high-energy performance that featured treble-high guitar with occasional distortion, proving again that Jonathan felt freer now than ever to experiment, even with a sound similar to that of the original Modern Lovers. Apart from cover versions of 'Hang On Sloopy', 'Tallahassee Lassie' and a driving 'Louie Louie', complete with a piercing, fuzz-coated solo, the set included new songs such as 'Take Me Off the Shelf' and 'Not Yet Three'. Perhaps the most surprising choice of the night was the encore, 'Pablo Picasso'. Not a song that Jonathan had played much since 1973, here it appeared in particularly raw form, with a twin-guitar ferocity courtesy of the rhythm playing of Billy Cole, who, a member of John Felice's Real Kids, played a few gigs with Jonathan at this time – there is a fiery coda reminiscent of the original Modern Lovers' performances of the song. This 'Picasso', although lyrically slightly different, exists on the same strung-out riff, repeated clinically and with dedication, punctuated by bursts of lead guitar. The applause that greeted it was half incredulous, half ecstatic.

While in New York Jonathan was interviewed by Kristine McKenna on 22 May at the Gramercy Park Hotel. This piece was eventually to appear in *New York Rocker* two years later. Jonathan is forthcoming and forthright here about his philosophy and lifestyle, emphasizing his desire to be true to himself, to take pleasure in nature, beauty and affection but not to run away from pain –instead to face it and conquer it. His reward for this is the ability to write his songs, which are founded in real feeling, and the love that flows back from his audience as a result. New York is electric but also weird and miserable; in Los Angeles the people can be 'bland on the surface and angry inside'; Jonathan loves Maine because of the 'nature and silence'. The last time he cried was that afternoon – a band had been playing Beatles songs in the park, and he was watching a beautiful girl. (As a footnote to this, David Robinson remembers sitting in a bar with Jonathan and seeing him start to cry when 'The Long and Winding Road' played on the jukebox.) Kristine McKenna asks him if he sees himself as 'a man with a mission' and he, while not thinking the evangelical inference appropriate, agrees: his mission is to entertain and inspire people to dance purely by expressing his own feelings.

Back home in Maine Jonathan was now playing about once a week in family restaurants and similarly unconventional venues, and sometimes he would invite his parents. Spare time was spent working out and reading.

By autumn Jonathan had decided that, after another period of consolidation and experimentation on his own, it was time once again to get a full-time band together. Despite his solo live work, he had been rehearsing and recording with other musicians for a while and, with Ellie and Curly firmly in place, the line-up was already nearly complete. The problem, perhaps predictably, was finding the right person to fill the all-important position of drummer – someone who could play at low volume without dragging the beat – and it was not until September, after a couple of experiments had ended in failure, that Jonathan discovered Michael Guardabascio.

Acting on a recommendation, Jonathan phoned Michael, introduced himself and told him that he was looking for a drummer to complete his new band – a band that was by now due to travel to Los Angeles in two weeks to record an album and tour locally. An 'audition' took place – consisting simply of Michael's percussive backing to Jonathan's vocals – after which Michael was informed that the job was his and that they left on Tuesday. Later that night Jonathan came back to his house and presented him with his ticket.

There had been another position to fill that week, though; Ellie's singing partner, Liz Does, was no longer with the band and a new backing vocalist was needed urgently. Jonathan told Ellie that he was looking for someone who really enjoyed singing and who had good rhythm, and she came up with Beth Harrington, who happened to live downstairs from her – the two singing together would become known as the Rockin' Robins.

This new band would still be called the Modern Lovers (Jonathan would continue to use the name until the end of the eighties) but would perform very little of the material associated with the earlier incarnations and would also forsake their four-man line-up – signs that Jonathan had put real distance now between himself and his early days. There would be a fluidity to the new outfit, too; having already been through a couple of drummers and a backing vocalist they would, at various times, use second guitarists, another female singer, a horn player and the keyboards of Ken Forfia, as well as surviving temporary absences of almost all the permanent members at one time or another. The most significant change in the band's sound was the replacement of the second guitar of the conventional rock outfit with the vocals of Ellie and Beth, vocals that would be given the prominence of a front-line instrument. This was another signal that his confrontational approach had been consigned to the past – the unity of an all-male band with its 'traditionally male' instrumentation had been replaced by the variety of a male/female approach and a more 'complete' sound. The female presence in the band mirrored that of Gail's in his emotional life and on occasion would be used to give a voice to it.

The tour of California lasted three weeks and gave the band's members the chance to gel as a live unit before they set off on the series of wider-ranging US dates that would follow in the new year. Between tours, though, a session had been arranged at Capitol Recording Studios in Los Angeles. Here, once more, the band tried to record Jonathan's new album – and again nothing came of the attempts.

A substantial amount of material recorded at Capitol has never emerged in any form: 'Don't Change Your Ways for Me', 'Are You Feeling Good?', 'I See What's Underneath', 'I Can't Stand to See People with Their Feelings Hurt', 'I Love Her Little Body' and 'Dick Gregory'.

Among these songs is at least one that stands with Jonathan's very best: 'I See What's Underneath'. Here, for the first and only time to date, he talks about his parents and brother in his lyrics. Each character in the song exists in two forms: as their current selves, with only hints of the way they are, and as children, their youthful essence and potential as people laid bare. Between the twin impressions a whole character and developing personality is sketched, as each life is lived (and the living takes its toll), with its strength and vulnerability, passion and innocence, pride and compromise. The result is truth and poignancy and, like 'That Five-Year-Old Feeling', a tragedy of omission in Jonathan's recorded output.

These new songs were just part of a seemingly endless supply, inspired by an equally limitless source of experiences and emotions that flowed at least as freely as it had always done. Michael Guardabascio remembers one occasion when the band was on tour and Jonathan was struck by the echo in the stairwell of a hotel. Grouping his musicians on the steps, he started to write a song on the spot. On other occasions he would write while walking down the street or wake, inspired, in the middle of the night – whenever a song came to him he would seize the moment.

Back on the East Coast in February 1981 the band played the Psyche Delly in Washington – a gig reviewed by Geoffrey Himes in the *Washington Post*. At one point during the evening some members of the audience started laughing at the beginning of a song. Jonathan stopped the band and said: 'I heard some laughter. Who thinks I'm being sarcastic?' To the responding shouts of the crowd he replied: 'Well, you're wrong. I don't do that.' Ellie and Beth sang 'doo-wahs' and clapped their hands, and Jonathan wore a loose white sweater and an unbuttoned shirt. It was as if the eighties and the fifties had somehow become knotted together in time.

The year 1981 was to be a frustrating one for the new band. Living something of a hand-to-mouth existence on their return from tour they shuttled between Boston and San Francisco. While in Berkeley they made another ill-fated attempt, at Fantasy Studios, to record *Jonathan Sings!* Although the pattern of the band's movements was similar to that of their immediate predecessors they did not benefit from anything like the same financial stability that the second form ation of the Modern Lovers had enjoyed and, as the months went by, became increasingly unhappy with what they saw as the failure of their record label, Beserkley, to come up either with sufficient live work or with realistic plans for the release of a new album.

At the end of another trip from Boston to San Francisco the band's dissatisfaction became all too clear, and Jonathan, who had initially been willing to give the people at Beserkley the benefit of the doubt, having worked with them and known them as friends for so long, now decided that it was time a change was made. Within a week he had signed a new manager, Ken Baker.

In the autumn of 1981 demos were recorded in New York that were to form the basis of *Jonathan Sings!*, but this album, although finished by early 1982, would not actually be released until 1983. Through the connection with Andy Paley the demos were brought to the attention of Seymour Stein, head of Sire Records. Sire was a part of the Warner Brothers empire – ironic considering the earlier unfruitful relationship with the original Modern Lovers – and with Stein's approval of the demos Jonathan would now begin the second of three associations with the company.

*Jonathan Sings!* was finally recorded at Sunset Studios in Burbank. However, much of the material taped at the sessions would not be used. Geoff Travis, head of Rough Trade, the organization that would later release the album in the UK, remembers hearing some of the discarded tracks in Burbank and thinking they were 'sensational' and even more commercial than the album that would eventually appear – itself probably the most 'conventional'-sounding of Jonathan's albums thus far. A lot of these tracks were alternative ver- sions of songs that would appear on the album, but rejected takes also included a vibrant 'Up in the Sky Sometime' and a forceful 'I See What's Underneath'.

When the album finally appeared in 1983 it was Jonathan's most polished, obviously 'produced' album ever. The songs, too, were extremely strong, and the musical backing given to them versatile, passionate and accomplished. With major label backing, good reviews on its release and a band that was by now more than ready to promote it, it should have been, in terms of sales, Jonathan's most successful piece of work to date. However, no single was taken from it in the USA, and Warner Brothers in the UK did not even release it, leaving Rough Trade to pick it up the following year. What could have been a great opportunity was missed by the record company.

The sound on *Jonathan Sings!* is very smooth, with drums and bass tight together and an almost mellow sheen to the backing vocals. Keyboards are used sparingly and generally mixed down – but there is something a little too 'tasteful' about them. Jonathan's guitar, too, is not always enough in evidence, and the reverb on his vocals takes away a little of their directness. The overall sound may have been too 'professional' for Jonathan's liking (re-recorded versions of 'That Summer Feeling' and 'The Neighbors' would feature on subsequent albums), but it highlights the backing vocals and the way they can build up and slow down a song, and the arrangements, despite being less direct than before, certainly allow the songs to breathe. At a late stage Jonathan had tried to change the production by bringing in Josef Marc (who would later make live appearances and record with him), but by then it was way too late and the rescue attempt was only partially successful.

For an album that had been so long in the making, however, there is nothing stale or forced here – a lot of the material was different from that of the initial attempts to record it in 1979 and 1980 – and the presence of a band that now combined experience and new blood gives the performances a real vitality. Moreover Jonathan was experiencing, for the first time, genuine personal happiness, having finally achieved with Gail the loving relationship that he had always needed. As a result, drawing inspiration from that love, he is freer than ever to identify and draw together the other aspects of his life that, together, make his happiness complete. Occasionally, though, he would still want to talk about some of the things that work against his happiness. From this point onwards, such a mixture would form a common pattern on Jonathan's albums.

The opening song, 'That Summer Feeling', is a celebration of the spontaneity of youth and its strength of feeling in reaction to the purest and simplest stimuli. It's also a reminder, however, of the importance of hanging on, in adulthood, to this ability to make such responses; without it people become bitter and nostalgic for things that never were. Jonathan lays out the intention behind his attempts to recapture childhood in his songs: far from wanting to return to his youth, he wants to bring back its awareness and instinctiveness and embed them in lifelong adulthood.

'This Kind of Music' is Jonathan's revolutionary rock-and-roll manifesto. It reduces that music to its most elemental – instruments that are barely functional, sometimes broken, a card-table for a drum kit, maybe even unaccompanied singing – and then says that sometimes even this is too much, that the music should be allowed to disappear completely, leaving behind only the expression of its essence: dance. By now music exists in its purest possible form, solely as inspiration.

'Those Conga Drums', with booming semi-acoustic guitar and pounding drums way in the distance, reaches back to 1973, with Jonathan in Venice Beach, the original Modern Lovers disintegrating around him. Music is salvation here again, and it is music that is both simple and full of feeling able to speak to anyone.

'You're the One for Me' deals with the inevitability of the coming together of Jonathan and Gail – nothing else could have happened from the moment she was born. The certainty with which Jonathan looks back is equal to the certainty with which he had looked forward on the songs from the 1974 studio session; the movement in both directions across time being equally significant and equally predictable.

On 'When I'm Walking' Jonathan describes this most completely natural expression of his relationship with the world: no windscreen, no train window, no metal chassis, nothing between him and his environment. The lyrics and music – including some of Jonathan's best guitar work – finally give way to foot-stomping as the song ends and becomes one with its subject.

In May Jonathan had been interviewed by his neighbour, George Parsons, for *Option* magazine. He had talked about the secret of magic in music, how it is experienced through the free expression of feeling, without it having to be willed. On these occasions Jonathan gets a chill down the spine and starts to cry, he said. To illustrate this he described an incident that had occurred the day before. While talking to one of the members of the band Green On Red outside the college at which he was to perform later in the evening, a car pulled up. Inside were a young man and woman who had asked for his autograph and requested that he sing 'That Summer Feeling' for them. With an audience of three Jonathan did just that, 'painting the picture for them'. As he sang he felt the chill come over him, and he knew that they shared the feeling. Knowing that the magic of a moment like this was the summit of his art he was filled with 'spirit' and 'love for life'.

# 8 I'M JUST BEGINNING TO LIVE

THE new Modern Lovers played many live dates to promote *Jonathan Sings!* and the gigs were enthusiastically and appreciatively received. Apart from traditional rock-and-roll gigs, they continued Jonathan's policy of playing unusual venues. Due to play one evening at a club called the Fast Lane on the Jersey coast, the band arrived early and decided to pass the afternoon by the sea. As Michael Guardabascio recalls, 'Jonathan was out there serenading the old Jewish ladies on the beach' – and they loved him. They knew that his desire to entertain them was sincere and picked up on it straight away – both parties had a great time.

Geoff Travis at Rough Trade, the pioneering independent label born at the start of punk, had loved the album at first hearing and had decided to license it from Seymour Stein. Stein had told him that the UK arm of Warner Brothers had decided not to release it, regarding it as unlikely to make enough money. Travis, on the other hand, thought it 'the best record Jonathan had made for a long, long time'.

On its British release in 1984 the album received good reviews, just as it had in the USA, and Rough Trade went on to release 'That Summer Feeling' as a single – with more cover art by Jonathan, this time depicting a rural roadside scene.

In June 1984 Jonathan and the Modern Lovers began a European tour. Some of the dates on the British leg, including one at the Hammersmith Palais in London, were as special guests of the successful Scottish post-punk band Orange Juice. The members of Orange Juice, their leader Edwyn Collins in particular, were longstanding fans of Jonathan's, even naming one of their albums, *You Can't Hide Your Love Forever*, after a line from his song 'Hi Dear'.

For Ellie, this European tour was 'one of the hardest I've ever done, but it was probably one of the best. I think we were an unusual rock band touring – this reputation bands have for sleeping with different people every night and doing drugs and stuff – it just wasn't like that!' Ellie's presence in the band gave Jonathan the opportunity to dramatize his songs, occasionally to provide a counterbalance to his own views and to put a feminine perspective on them. Her role was never purely that of a backing singer; she always added the extra dimension created by a real presence in the songs.

Part of the way through the tour Michael Guardabascio had to return home for personal reasons. Although they missed him, his absence did not cause a crisis and Jonathan did not bother trying to find a replacement – the band just played without a drummer. On this part of the tour, with only Jonathan's guitar and Curly's bass for backing, Ellie's role as contraster/harmonizer – musically, lyrically and as a woman singing together with a man – was particularly enhanced and particularly effective.

A new song performed at the Hacienda in Manchester, 'I Moved Away', is a further step towards Jonathan's goal of simplicity and the refining of life down to its fundamentals. 'All-night delicatessens' and 'rock bars that stay open all night' are forsaken for fields, snakes and desert, revealing a sensitivity to the environment that would grow over the coming years and a concern about its abuse that would emerge in his interviews. The song is the first about Jonathan's new home surroundings: firmly united now with Gail and her son Jason he had forsaken his native New England for the warmth of California and a house near the Sierra Nevada. The main reason he gave for this was the change of climate and the benefits it would bring to his family, but in a sense it was another example of him rejecting his past –

although, once again, he would not reject it completely and would continue to make regular return journeys to the scenes of his youth.

On 6 August Jonathan, backed by Ellie and Curly, played at Dingwalls, at Camden Lock in London. It was a hot summer night in a hip part of town and a sell-out. The club may even have been over-full – it certainly seemed that way with people jammed together: plenty of heat and little air. In the audience was Phil Kaufman, living in London at the time and keeping in touch with Jonathan as he has continued to do in the years since then. 'We keep writing to each other, Christmas cards and silly postcards from the road and things like that. When we're in the same town we always get together; we're good buddies. We run and scream and hug each other.' Also there was Glen Matlock: 'I actually met him up at Dingwalls when he played there. I was out of my head and I was trying to be nice, and I said: "*You started punk rock!*", and he was like: "Well, don't blame me!" You know how these things come out after a few brown ales! I think I got ushered out, actually.'

Jonathan was on particularly fine form that night, singing 'When I'm Walking' unaccompanied, turning down a request with a 'Fat chance!', shouting out the key changes for 'The Tag Game', a joyful celebration of play, improvising across a sea of styles on an instrumental version of 'Lover Please' and reciting a couple of tiny poems, one of which, 'The Little Green and White Wrapper', would later become a fully fledged song, 'Chewing Gum Wrapper'.

The crowd was noisy but appreciative, with occasional insensitivity overcome by a general goodwill. After an encore the show seemed over and the DJ began playing records. The audience refused to let it end, however, shouting and drumming on the floor until Jonathan finally returned, without either a band or a guitar, and began to recite 'Shirin and Fahrad', a retelling of the story of Romeo and Juliet set in ancient Egypt. Some of the audience, expecting a humorous end to the evening and determined to have it, tried to inject comedy into a song that has a serious intent, a song that needs smiles of affection, not bellows of laughter. Even for Jonathan, used to dealing with insensitivity, this was too much and he was unable to hide his disappointment with their reaction, cutting short his performance to explain that people who don't relate properly to him shouldn't come to his shows and that it might, therefore, be best if he changed the kind of venues at which he played. Jonathan then resumed the song and the crowd was silent to the end – but he never played Dingwalls again.

The end of the tour saw the end, too, of Curly's full-time association with Jonathan. He had always hoped that they would tour abroad together and had achieved that ambition. But at the end of a long period of playing much the same material at smoky one-off gigs he had decided it was time for a change. Curly would continue to be a close friend of Jonathan's, though, and would later return to record and play live with him. 'We see each other regularly, because we live close together – we'll be friends for the rest of our lives . . . He really is unique . . . someone you can trust, and he's never, ever going to trick anybody or cheat anybody. He's just not that kind of person – he trusts completely . . . I've really enjoyed all the bands I've been in with him.'

Gerard Malanga's and Victor Bockris's definitive history of the Velvet Underground, *Up-tight*, had been published by this time. It featured a short account by Jonathan of the band's chosen amplification and effects pedals and the different guitars that Lou Reed used with their modifications. Malanga recalls asking Jonathan to contribute. 'I did an interview with him, I think it was by mail actually, and he also sent me a drawing, dissecting Lou's guitar.' The drawing was not used, but Jonathan's account is sharp and detailed, revealing what must have been an intimate knowledge of the Velvets' instrumentation over a substantial proportion of their time together, together with a precise memory of it.

A lot of the new songs played on the European tour were to appear on Jonathan's next album, *Rockin' and Romance*, which, although recorded in 1984, would not appear until 1985. When it was released, it was on Rough Trade; Geoff Travis had decided that he wanted to work with Jonathan and had made a deal with him that would cover his next two albums.

The first sessions for Rough Trade took place at the old RCA studios in Los Angeles where Elvis Presley had recorded. The idea behind this was that all the old valve equipment still installed there would enable the tracks to capture an authentic vintage sound. Problems arose, however, when the painstaking professionalism of the engineer rubbed up against Jonathan's spontaneity. Geoff lent a hand for a couple of days, but the experience proved frustrating for all concerned, and eventually Jonathan's old friend Andy Paley was called upon. As Geoff recalls, he proved to be the ideal choice. 'He really understood Jonathan. He's a great musician, he plays lots of instruments, and he became the producer and did a very good job. Andy's musical knowledge is incredible, and it probably matches Jonathan's to some degree, so he was really able to translate what Jonathan wanted in a way that not many people would be able to . . . He knows about doo-wop and all the rest of it, which Jonathan could really empathize with, and he's quite a maverick producer, which probably suits Jonathan.'

The musical backing on *Rockin' and Romance* was Jonathan's starkest yet, in marked contrast to *Jonathan Sings!* Apart from a whole choir of backing vocalists (including Ellie Marshall and the first appearance of many by Ned Claflin, ex-member of the Baltimores, the a cappella group immortalized here in song), the instrumentation was very simple: Jonathan on guitars, Michael Guardabascio on drums and Andy Paley with a bizarre combination of 'toy piano' and 'drum solo'.

At the beginning of these new sessions, there were more problems as the band tried various arrangements and different rooms (including the kitchen of engineer Paul Emery) without anything really working. (Some of these demos, nevertheless, are rather fine, with a warm vocal sound, some different arrangements and songs that would not appear on the final album.) Eventually, after three weeks of rehearsals that had failed to bring the expected results, a break was called and, with the exception of Jonathan and Michael, the band headed off for a weekend in San Francisco. The two remaining members decided to go over to the studio, start playing and see what happened. The result was that the whole rhythm section for the album was recorded in that one weekend, in about six hours of work, an experience that Michael will never forget. 'That was a special moment . . . it was probably the height of my musical experience. It just clicked; we had the feeling . . . Jonathan was standing right in front of me, I had one of those little baffles in front of the kick drum . . . and we just recorded the whole thing, staring at each other all the time.'

The songs travel the length and breadth of Jonathan's world, from eulogies to his heroes ('Vincent Van Gogh', 'Walter Johnson', 'The Baltimores') to his love for Gail and her influence on his life ('I Must Be King', 'Now Is Better Than Before'), episodes from his youth ('Down in Bermuda', 'The Fenway'), dreams of the stars ('Up in the Sky Sometime', 'The UFO Man') and then the *really* important things ('The Beach', 'My Jeans', 'Chewing Gum Wrapper').

The musical variety comes from a mixture of acoustic and semi-acoustic guitars and male and female vocal harmonies (sometimes in three parts) and from the contrast between drums that drive one song without pausing for breath and are then nearly or totally absent in the next. Other highlights are the occasional snatches of melodic lead guitar and unexpected musical sections, such as the coda to 'The Fenway' with its ethereal vocals and poignant acoustic guitar. Musically and lyrically this is a consistently stimulating album, ranging wide but unified by its embrace of simple unsung pleasures and its capturing of the spirit of timeless rock and roll. Two of its stand-out tracks feature what might seem particularly unusual subjects: 'Walter Johnson' and 'Chewing Gum Wrapper'. 'Walter Johnson' is a tribute to the eponymous baseball star. With just his own occasional acoustic guitar for accompaniment, Jonathan races through the words but leaves pauses between the verses to ensure that his message gets across. You do not need to know anything about baseball, though, to understand the song – it is about honour, strength of character and love. Jonathan audibly clenches his teeth around the line 'a game, it was supposed to be just a game' – there is nothing trivial or fanciful here. 'Chewing Gum Wrapper' expands the poem 'The Little Green and White Wrapper' and comes up with a homage to a most unlikely kind of beauty: a piece of rubbish lying in the dirt. What strikes Jonathan is the unique quality of its colours; soaked by the rain and then dried up by the sun they seem to come from a different spectrum. He knows he's behaving like a bum by picking it up, he knows most people won't understand, but he needs to try to explain his love – there's a beauty there that needs to be expressed.

In breaks between sessions for the album the band members would go outside and stand in a circle. Ned Claflin and Tom Nelson of the Baltimores would start singing an old rock-and-roll song and point round the circle in turn, until everyone had joined in. Sometimes these musical 'refreshments' would go on for hours.

Although both Ellie and Michael would be involved in the recording of *It's Time for Jonathan Richman and the Modern Lovers*, and both have gone on to play live with Jonathan in later years, the band that had toured Europe in 1984 effectively ceased full-time activity with Curly's departure. For Michael, the experience had brought both musical satisfaction and a friendship that will endure. 'I've played with a lot of people, but Jonathan is one of the very, very few people with whom there's a chemistry and a telepathy that gets developed over time. When he, all of a sudden, changes his mood, I know it instantly – within a split second. Sometimes you can anticipate what mood he will be in – all of a sudden you hear him playing a certain figure and doing it a certain way and . . . you say: "Here he goes. OK, we're into this." I love that . . . It was incredibly tiring, but it was the music that kept you going . . . Jonathan is an amazingly loyal friend, a true friend. Even though he lives three thousand miles away from me and I may not speak to him for a month at a time, it's like you speak to him every day. As soon as the phone rings, he calls from somewhere out there: "Hey, Mikey, what's happening?" and bingo, we're into it.'

The dissolution of this band had a much more relaxed and natural feel to it than those of Jonathan's first two line-ups of Modern Lovers, and this would set a new pattern. From now on he would be able to dip into (and out of) an expanding pool of collaborators, all of whom were happy with the casualness of the arrangement. Long gone were the days of campaigns to be fought.

His next regular gigs would show another change of style with the return of Asa Brebner, this time on electric guitar, and a full-time, but temporary, role as drummer for Andy Paley. Andy, first as a friend and friendly rival, then as a part-time collaborator, had always been a part of Jonathan's musical life, but, with *Rockin' and Romance*, its successor *It's Time For Jonathan Richman and the Modern Lovers* and gigs together until 1988, the two now enjoyed a period of even closer association. (Music was not the only interest shared between the two, though. They also had a mutual love of exploring new places – both of them enjoying the process of searching out the best food, checking out the atmosphere and meeting the locals.)

In the spring of 1985 Jonathan's and Gail's daughter Jenny was born. Jonathan, for whom domesticity has always been restrictive, was never likely to be good on the practicalities of child care, and so it would prove – a subject he would go on to discuss in 'My Little Girl's Got a Full-Time Daddy Now' from the 1996 album, *Surrender to Jonathan*. But he loved his daughter from the very start and would soon be saying how much he missed her when touring abroad.

That summer Jonathan undertook a series of European dates with Andy and Asa. Jonathan was in a solidly electric phase, and this band was to produce some of the noisiest, most driven music since the original Modern Lovers. Some of the songs were extended far beyond their original limits, with Jonathan given the chance for occasional lengthy pieces of lead work. Instrumental versions of standards such as 'Money' and 'La Bamba' had become an integral part of every live set and would often be the starting point of a show, a chance for the band to loosen up and an early burst of energy to propel proceedings into life. With Jonathan playing most of the solos, Asa would concentrate on rhythm guitar but would sometimes also play bass lines and occasionally provide his own fluid, classic lead breaks. Andy's drum kit was tiny, but it was pounded and battered into providing rhythms that radiated primitive rock-and-roll life, the perfect engine for a raw twin-guitar drive.

While in Germany in June the band was filmed performing at Hamburg's Markethalle and Jonathan was also interviewed. Part of the interview is carried out in song. The band approach the camera – Jonathan is singing and playing guitar – and they seat themselves on a bench. Asked about his daily regime, Jonathan improvises a rap over the R&B pattern that Andy is now picking out on the guitar and runs through the hours of the day, describing the way he breaks it down into sleep/rest time and work time: up at the crack of dawn, Jonathan can sometimes be back in bed by nine if things aren't going well, resurfacing later to try again – his facility for falling asleep at any time still very much a part of his life.

On 5 July the band played two sets at the Hammersmith Riverside Studios in London. As well as songs that would appear on *It's Time for Jonathan Richman and the Modern Lovers*, a couple of others were played that have never been released. 'Tell How You Feel' is a plea for emotional honesty – even at the cost of upsetting someone – and 'Let's Say We Just Met' is a romantic fantasy used for a serious purpose, detailing a way of eradicating the staleness that can creep into a relationship. Both of these songs are tightly argued from a perspective that refuses to accept that the everyday is necessarily banal, and they are melodic with strong rhythm guitar lines. Maybe they will surface at a later date, but for the moment they are more buried treasure.

While in England in July, Jonathan was interviewed on BBC Radio One by Janice Long, their discussion punctuated by some of Jonathan's favourite records. Jonathan stood up and danced in the studio while the records were played and sang along both to the lyrics and the instrumental parts. During the course of the interview he recalled the exact dates of the three occasions when he saw the Lovin' Spoonful perform live and said that, despite not being good with names, he is great with numbers and can, without having to make any effort, recall old phone numbers from the third and fourth grades. Radio interviews, he said, are far preferable to the written kind because the listener can take into account the tone of voice of the interviewee as well as the words and can make a judgement, therefore, that is not reliant just on information filtered through a third party. Jonathan was his own DJ for much of the interview, introduced his selections with massive enthusiasm and pointed out particular points of interest to look out for. His listening at the time included Rough Trade's African artists, Brazilian compilations and American Indian music, some styles of which rely purely on singing and percussion. He said he had been to intertribals, where the different tribes from the desert states gather in the open and produce music that has sent chills up his spine. As the interview progressed it transpired that most of the records he chose are from 1962 – but in terms of his own music even these were too sophisticated in their recording techniques to provide a blueprint for him; he wanted to make music that is cruder still, a direction he underlined by emphasizing his current dismissal of the bass guitar in the studio as well as when playing live. Jonathan's record collection, despite his varied interests, was minimal; he 'doesn't like to keep too many things around'. The interview ended with an expression of his ever-increasing interest in conservation and his concern, in particular, about the destruction of the rain forests, a process that he felt should be halted immediately. (Back in 1983, while being interviewed by George Parsons, Jonathan had expressed similar concerns, announcing that he was to play at a 'blockade' organized by a group called Earth First up in the Siskyos Range in Oregon. The event had been arranged to try to prevent the building of a road through sacred Indian ground and 'one of the last wilderness areas of the Abominable Snowman'.)

After leaving the UK, Jonathan returned to the USA, where he played in California and the Midwest – including two shows with John Cale, one of which saw an appearance by Sterling Morrison – before heading over to the East Coast. (Cale has remained friendly with Jonathan over the years, their meetings since the failure of the 1973 sessions having, he says, 'a convivial atmosphere, which I was glad restored a certain balance to things'. He has also, as did Sterling Morrison, received Jonathan's 'funny postcards' from 'all over the world'.)

After the USA the band went up to Canada and then on to Australia, where Don Spindt took over from Andy on drums. This almost continuous touring would become a pattern for Jonathan in the mid- to late eighties as he moved repeatedly through North America, Europe, Australia and Japan in a schedule that sometimes resulted in him visiting countries twice in one year.

Although not actually released until 1986, *It's Time for Jonathan Richman and the Modern Lovers* was recorded in 1985 and, like its predecessor, was on the Rough Trade label and produced by Andy Paley.

During the sessions for this album Andy had a crowd of people in the studio, dancing and reacting to the music – the technology was sophisticated enough for none of this to interfere with the actual recording. The result was that Jonathan, freed from the conventional restrictions of these situations, could treat the record more as a live performance and be inspired, in turn, by the effects of his music on other people. The only problem was keeping him within the range of his microphone, as his dancing would often lead him away.

*It's Time for Jonathan Richman and the Modern Lovers* features a similar line-up of musicians to *Rockin' and Romance* and similar production from Andy. Once again there is no bass, but this time Jonathan's guitar work is augmented by that of Asa and Andy, and there is in addition occasional use of Jonathan's saxophone talents (maturing nicely now), accordion from Ned Claflin and, in a seemingly impossible attempt to upstage his previous credit of 'Toy Piano', Andy Paley on 'Chimes by Mattel'.

The songs run the now familiar Richman gamut, covering romance, the past and its association with the present and pure enjoyment of the simplest of life's pleasures, but they do so with a mixture of humour and seriousness that implies a complexity of vision that may not immediately be apparent to the casual listener. 'It's You', 'This Love of Mine' and 'Just About Seventeen' are all songs that seem to lie on the edge of the memory, as if they are long-forgotten 'pop classics', songs from the very birth of rock and roll, when music was in its purest state and best able to handle the purest emotions. 'Let's Take a Trip' bursts with the feeling of freedom that inspired it, whereas 'Neon Sign' flits between the past and the present, distilling the essence of both. (On the latter the inspirations for 'Roadrunner' and 'Ride Down on the Highway' are shown to be still inspirations, but the loneliness that once made them seem all-important is now gone.) 'Double Chocolate Malted' was a spur-of-the-moment creation, improvised in the recording studio, from Jonathan's initial shout of just those three words. Andy Paley replied: 'Yeah, yeah, yeah', the other backing vocalists joined in, and the song was born. 'Corner Store' is a straightforward plea for a rejection of the present in favour of the past – but not purely for the sake of nostalgia; this is also a qualitative judgement. What has happened to one particular shop, one set of trees, one rejection of wood in favour of concrete is part of something larger, something that needs to be stopped. 'The Desert' echoes 'Neon Sign' in its arousal of feelings from the past: the barrenness of the landscape clears the way for a flow of impressions from time gone by, some forgotten from youth, some perhaps from somewhere else. 'Yo Jo Jo' is a manic R&B instrumental based on the Surfaris' 'Wipe Out' and features the first use of distortion on a Jonathan Richman recording since those of the original Modern Lovers. 'When I Dance', with its hypnotic pattern of minor chords, conjures up a transformation of reality that is not drug induced and uncontrollable but self-induced and natural, an expression of the power of music in movement. The version of 'Shirin and Fahrad' is not entirely unaccompanied, as it was when performed on stage. Acoustic guitars and sometimes just a beat on the guitar body provide a sparse setting for this story of true love and its tragic end . . . Or is it the end? 'Ancient Long Ago' takes memories of 'The Desert' and the story of 'Shirin and Fahrad' and suggests a link between the present and the past, ending the album on a similar note to that of 'I Hear You Calling Me' from *Back in Your Life*. Ned Claflin's accordion sounds like the wind blowing across the years, and Ellie Marshall's vocals conjure up a spirit unaffected by death; eternity, spirituality and love are bound together.

In February 1986 Jonathan was the subject of a half-hour show called 'Cutting Edge' on MTV during which, as well as playing some of his new songs, he was interviewed. Asked about the pleasure he gets from live shows, he replied that it depends very much on the audience. Sometimes people hide their feelings and look around at everyone else to gauge how they are supposed to react, and sometimes they're not afraid to let their feelings show – and that is the difference between a live audience and a dead one, Jonathan maintained.

In March, after live gigs in the USA, Jonathan was back in Europe. By now Asa had left the band again, going on to form his own, Idle Hands and Asa Brebner and Friends. Like most of Jonathan's musical associates, though, he keeps in touch, remaining a good friend. He would be more than happy to work with Jonathan once more. 'I'd love to! He's such a wild man and does what he wants to do. It's terrifying!'

Andy was still very much in the band, but this time he was playing acoustic guitar – as was Brennan Totten who, as well as being a musician, would also become Jonathan's regular producer from the next album until the mid-nineties. Brennan had first met Jonathan while playing in a blues band in Northern California. Unknown to him, Jonathan had come into the club to check out his playing. Some months later, around eight o'clock in the morning, Brennan was at home feeding his daughter when Jonathan walked through his front door and began singing 'The UFO Man'. Reaching the chorus, he said: 'Your turn! You sing!' Brennan did just that, and when Jonathan heard the results he said: 'Oh, you can sing, too', and walked back out of the door. Not long afterwards the call came, and Brennan became a Modern Lover.

He and Jonathan played some gigs as a duo, and then Andy was asked to join in. Brennan and Andy met for the first time in a hotel room in Boulder, Colorado. They went through some songs together and two hours later the three of them played their first show as a band. They were to do little formal rehearsing for any of their live work: sometimes Jonathan would ask them to come up with a special vocal arrangement, and this might be constructed in a hotel room, but most of the songs' development would occur during live performances, leading to some special moments, as Andy recalls. 'He likes the accidents and the weird things that happen on stage. What he'll do is he'll attach himself to one thing. Let's say something just happened, you're playing a song and somebody just did something, Jonathan'll give you one of those big smiles and, later on, when you get off stage, he'll say: "Man, when you did that in such and such, remember that, because that was great."'

As well as having the two acoustic guitars backing him (they were played into microphones – no pick-ups), Jonathan was now playing a lot of saxophone, particularly in the introductions to songs, for solos and in instrumentals such as 'Egyptian Reggae'. The line-up of this band had a surprising versatility: Andy and Brennan would provide vocal harmonies and play bass lines as well as chords and, when it came to percussion, either they would slap the bodies of their guitars or Jonathan would stomp his feet, and the audience would create the rest by clapping along. Without a guitar round his neck, Jonathan was free to dance along to the music – which he did energetically – provoking delighted applause. Unexpected key changes (as unexpected for Andy and Brennan as for the audience) would be prefaced by a shout of 'F!' or 'G!', and the sound of a drum solo would mysteriously appear as if from nowhere. On closer examination it would turn out to be Andy's or Brennan's hands beating a tattoo on the wood of a reversed acoustic. Visually, too, the band were striking: Andy and Brennan, both with blond hair, had matching red shirts which they would wear each night, contrasting with Jonathan's dark hair and maybe a turquoise shirt. The idea was Andy's and Brennan's, but Jonathan was struck with it, too.

While on the Spanish leg of the European tour Jonathan and the band were filmed for the *Arsenal* television programme. The live footage shows Jonathan in his element playing to a whooping audience of all ages, children and adults, who sing along in English – and in Spanish to 'La Bamba'. Some studio tracks are also featured, with specially shot video footage. The highlight of these is 'Ice Cream Man', which shows Jonathan, band and friends sitting down to a huge meal. Here Jonathan tries his hand at the job of waiter, spills the contents of his tray over Andy and is rewarded with a swinging 'punch' from the irate diner which sends him sprawling. Asked in the interview what he misses most about childhood, Jonathan replies that, at the age of nine or ten, after dinner in the evening everyone used to run outside to play ball or tag – now that his friends are over thirty they sit and drink coffee or beer, watch television or read the paper, and none of this is his idea of fun.

On 23 March the band played at London's Town and Country Club, which was full to capacity with a highly appreciative audience producing the perfect atmosphere and inspiring a wonderful performance. By now, with several gigs behind them, the band were really tight and the harmonies perfectly balanced. Jonathan was so pleased with the show that he sent Andy a tape of it as a souvenir.

While in England Jonathan was interviewed once more, this time by *Blitz* magazine. Being on the verge of losing his voice, much of the interview was conducted through a process of spoken questions and written replies – fortunately Jonathan has the capacity for loquaciousness on paper. Continuing to espouse conservationist causes, he expresses a desire for the reinstatement of wolves in the wild in England and cougars and grizzly bears in California. Turning to fashion, Jonathan proclaims himself a fan of sweaters, corduroy trousers, shirts with buttons that you can undo when it gets hot – and T-shirts for a change. Colours are aqua and white, orange and white, dark blue, pink and white. The best clothes are the timeless ones, 'so it looks like a guy on a pirate ship could have worn 'em, or an ancient desert guy'. Jonathan talks, too, here about his memories of past lives: 'Flashback-type memories of what feel like the sixteen hundreds, ancient desert days (I can't say for sure how old) and little feelings of things way old, like Atlantis or something.' To him, things like reincarnation and extra-sensory perception are not supernatural, they are just another part of the natural world. Asked if he would like his videos to get heavy rotation on MTV and make him a star, he says that he would. His response to the question of whether he will play rock and roll for ever is: 'I guess so.'

Jonathan was back playing shows in the USA at the end of 1986 and early 1987. At first Andy was still involved and, by this stage, there was even more of an emphasis on unorthodox percussion, as Brennan recalls. 'By the time we got back to the States, we were deeply involved in hammering on things! Stages, guitars, amplifiers, whatever we could get our hands on.'

When Andy, who had other commitments and had been available only in a temporary capacity – and playing for the sheer pleasure of it – left, Jonathan decided to hire a full-time drummer. After, as usual, trying a few people who did not work out, Jonathan came across Johnny Avila.

Jonathan had been looking for a 'one-drum deal', as Brennan puts it, and Johnny was one of the very few candidates who was happy with that. Also, as Brennan says: 'He had a certain quality that nobody else had . . . [He] was the only guy who could actually evoke that thundering fifties/sixties [sound] . . . The guy was a genius.'

With Johnny recruited to play 'drum', Jonathan decided to take up electric guitar again, and Brennan did the same.

On 27 February this line-up played at the Chicago Folk Club to a cheering, foot-stomping audience keen to give as much as they took. The version of 'Pablo Picasso' that they heard here accommodated a new middle section in a minor key. This eliminated some of the song's initial harshness and replaced it with a plea for those men who worry about their looks not to do so any more because the example of Picasso shows that being 'no handsome lover boy' need not be a handicap in matters of the heart. 'Affection' prompted a curtailed digression about compulsive eating being sometimes a kind of starving – for love – and a request for 'Astral Plane' led to an explanation of why that and some of the other older songs are not played any more: not because Jonathan doesn't like them but because he *does* like them. 'I couldn't do it for my own mother on her birthday. Don't you get it?' He has too much affection for the old songs to risk inferior versions of them – even songs he wrote recently only get performed if he he can put real feeling into them, and this is the reason he never uses set lists.

In June the band played at the Provincial Museum Theatre in Edmonton, Alberta, and Helen Metella in the *Edmonton Journal* described Jonathan 'breaking . . . off in mid-lyric to tell the parents of a weeping baby that they should definitely not leave the room because the infant was definitely not disturbing him'.

By now Rough Trade was experiencing the financial problems

that were soon to cause its downfall as a record label, and Jonathan's next album, *Modern Lovers '88* (although recorded in 1987), would be the first of many for the American independent label Rounder.

Geoff Travis had had enough money to put Jonathan's records out but, apart from trying to push 'That Summer Feeling' as a single, had not been able to invest in promoting them. Despite his absolute belief in his artist's abilities he had never really had the resources to raise his profile again to its seventies heights. This had not been a problem for Jonathan, though, who had been very happy with the label.

Now that their partnership was going to have to end, he knew that he wanted his next signing to be with a record company of similar integrity. Although primarily a 'roots' label, concentrating on styles such as bluegrass, rhythm and folk (and once more having little money to spare for promotion), Rounder would give Jonathan what Rough Trade had also given him – and what he most wanted – complete freedom to do what *he* wanted.

As well as a new record label, Jonathan also now had, with Andy Paley's other commitments growing, a new producer, Brennan Totten. Brennan and Jonathan were living near each other and, with their shared musical tastes and their on-road experience, he was the ideal candidate. It was to be a relationship that would produce some of Jonathan's best work.

# 9 PARTIES IN THE USA

THE new album, *Modern Lovers '88*, was recorded in Grass Valley, California, not far from Jonathan's home, in the autumn of 1987. It is truly a product of its environment, teeming with the life of the area: hot nights ripe for dancing and exploring, parties in the desert, farms overflowing with produce, lush vegetation, bike rides in the twilight. The production by Brennan Totten is suitably rich and full and it is hard to believe that there are only three musicians, with no overdubbing. The basic formula is a mixture of Jonathan's acoustic guitar, Brennan's electric, Johnny Avila's 'drum' and the harmonies of the backing vocals. The electric/acoustic mix is a potent one, rhythmic and resonant, and the absence once again of bass guitar goes unnoticed.

By the time recording began, the band were already well acquainted with the songs, having played them live many times, so there was no need for the long initial practice sessions of *Rockin' and Romance* and *It's Time for Jonathan Richman and the Modern Lovers*. Engineer Paul Emery had been an the road with them for half-a-dozen gigs in an attempt to capture the spontaneity of their live performances on tape and incorporate these recordings on the album, but the experiment did not really work and none of the material was used. In its place was the sound of a band playing live in the studio recreating that spontaneity. Brennan recalls: 'I think *Modern Lovers '88* sounds very direct. It was especially exciting for me actually to produce that record and to play on it. By the time we had finished mixing and sent it off to Rounder we were just astonished at what was happening, and I think it was due in a large part to Avila. I can't say enough about the guy. He was flat out easily the easiest person I have ever worked with – and not just because of it only being one drum. The guy had a huge amount to do with the artistic success of that album – although you can't go wrong with great songs.'

The opening track, 'Dancing Late at Night', takes place when most people are fast asleep – but Jonathan's wide awake. It's 3 a.m., he's out and he needs to dance. The sounds, lights and smells of the place where he's heading are conjured up in his mind and draw him along, alone . . . Four in the morning and now he's walking back through the deserted streets, still alone – and here the music slows, pausing to savour the stillness, before catching speed again, reprising the delights of dancing in the small hours. 'When Harpo Played His Harp' sets Harpo apart from the other Marx Brothers, his music the heavenly calm in the middle of a chaotic storm of manic comic invention. The song's melody is not sentimental, although it is pushed through with delight and pride. 'Gail Loves Me' says it all in the title. There are no other words, just a fat rhythm guitar sound, a soaring acoustic solo and stomping drums – music expressing love. 'African Lady', however, is a completely instrumental version of a song by the late Soolimon Ernest Rogie (S.E. for short), a singer/songwriter/guitarist from Sierra Leone whose 'palm wine' music Jonathan loves and who would play gigs with him in 1988. 'I Love Hot Nights' explodes out of the speakers with night-time heat, chatter and buzz, lights glowing out of the darkness. Two electric guitars and a single drum never sounded so huge. 'The Theme from Moulin Rouge' once again ends an album on a reflective note; with the melody line 'sung' to acoustic and electric guitar backing without percussion, Jonathan continues the story of his love for the romance of Paris and in the film's subject – Toulouse-Lautrec – brings another painter to join those already present in his songs: Cézanne, Picasso, Van Gogh and Vermeer.

The album's cover features a striking picture of Jonathan, saxophone in hand, outside a neon-lit motel, with twilight falling. The photograph was taken by Andy Paley. 'I think that's a beautiful photograph, I'm very proud of that, and I've never done anything like that in my whole life. It was sheer luck. But Jonathan called me up and said: "You took a beautiful photograph here." I liked the turquoise colour of his shirt . . . I liked the saxophone and the sunset . . . There's a neon sign . . . I was thinking of the song called "Neon Sign". I just remember thinking: This photo has got everything Jonathan Richman likes.'

By the beginning of 1988, when a new European tour began, Brennan Totten, in his new role as electric guitarist – playing mainly rhythm and occasional lead – was adding new dimensions to Jonathan's sound. Able to open up the existing song patterns when the occasion demanded, to establish a solid platform from which Jonathan could improvise and to move from that base towards simultaneous improvisation of his own, he was providing the magic mix of primitive rock and roll and imaginative splendour that Jonathan loves. At the same time Johnny Avila on 'drum' was providing the best possible rhythm accompaniment, ranging from the delicate to the mighty, while also being able to hold the sound tightly together when both guitarists ventured out on their own.

In London, on 6 March at the Town and Country Club, the band were really flying with their twin-engined guitar sound, particularly on songs such as 'Let's Take a Trip', 'Give Paris One More Chance' and a magnificently frantic 'Chewing Gum Wrapper'. The version of 'Vincent Van Gogh' now had a striking new couplet: 'His paintings, they had such soul/He had colours they didn't find till rock and roll'; on a quieter note, the version of 'Hospital' was prefaced with a little historical perspective, telling the audience how Jonathan had been obsessed with the girl who is the subject of the song and 'wouldn't let her alone . . . bugging her and pestering her'. At the end of the gig Jonathan announced that the band were returning to the USA the next day and threw some cards into the audience, asking anyone out there who was 'in love' to write to him.

Both Brennan and Johnny had recently been giving some thought to the idea of retiring from a life on the road and so, when they got home and Jonathan told them that he had decided it was time to return to touring on his own, it seemed like a good time to make the decision. By this time anyone playing with Jonathan knew what to expect on this score, and it was no longer a big deal, although both would obviously miss what they had enjoyed so much. Brennan, of course, would continue to be heavily involved in Jonathan's career as both producer and occasional studio musician.

For Jonathan, this last stint playing in bands had paved the way towards another of his periodic periods of renewal and reassessment, and his solo live appearances would be reflected this time in near-solo appearances in the studio.

In June he was back in England again for three consecutive nights at London's Mean Fiddler. A complete, if rather distant, version of 'She Cracked' was an unexpected delight on the first night, but it was the third night that really took off. Jonathan and the audience hit it off perfectly and the result was a stream of asides and anecdotes punctuating some impassioned singing and guitar-playing. During 'Egyptian Reggae' Jonathan spotted Soolimon Rogie who, having played an opening set, was standing at the side of the stage. Launching into the chords of 'African Lady', he invited him on stage to sing, which he did beautifully, exiting afterwards through the applauding crowd. The night's old song, 'Girlfriend', prompted a recollection from Jonathan of how it was not so much the paintings in the Museum of Fine Arts in Boston that used to bring him there so much as the college girls with their 'high-heeled leather boots and . . . suede handbags'. Jonathan, still at high school, had been most impressed. At the end of 'That Summer Feeling' a voice shouted 'I love you, Jonathan!', prompting him to tell the tale of the first time he ever heard Gail's voice, shouting 'We love you!' at a Modern Lovers' gig. Having by that time seen her face a few times in the crowd when the band played, to have her finally calling out to him had been a moment of pure magic. For the final section of 'Just About Seventeen' the audience did all the singing and Jonathan just danced; no band, no guitar, no vocal – pure joy.

After London it was off to Europe again, including Germany, France and Spain, before a trip to Canada and then back to the USA in November.

By the time of the sessions that would make up the majority of next year's album, *Jonathan Richman*, Jonathan had decided to try and create some of the intimacy of his current solo shows on vinyl as well. The musical backing here was to be his simplest yet. In fact he was pretty much the only musician, as Brennan remembers. 'That was as much Jonathan Richman as you can get on a record . . . All the percussion things that you hear come out of a cardboard box that Richman keeps in his basement. The damnedest things come out of that box! That triangle was quite a trial to record, we kept running into difficulties with the harmonics.'

When work had first begun on the record, however, a very different approach had been tried: a whole album's worth of material had been recorded with Jonathan being backed by Brennan on guitar, Curly on bass and the late Ron 'Wipe Out' Wilson on drums, and two of these tracks would in fact survive to make the final cut.

Although Brennan remembers it as 'wonderful, perfect music', when playing the tapes back later on Jonathan was unhappy with his playing. He decided that he would have to begin again – and that that would give him the opportunity to use a much sparser approach. It was not that the material somehow needed more intimacy than usual, just that in striving for the most effective way to present his songs this seemed, at the time, to be it. The result is a course of raw Richman with the minimum of extra flavouring: a smattering of percussion and a tiny portion of bass and drums.

The first track, 'Malagueña de Jojo', is Jonathan's variation on a traditional Spanish gypsy song often turned into this kind of improvised instrumental. Jonathan's semi-acoustic guitar is backed only by occasional foot-stamping, but he switches from pick-up to pick-up, slows the pace and accelerates again, picks and then strums, changing the mood from reflective to proud and creating a range of musical impressions like a sonic landscape. 'Fender Stratocaster' is of course not performed on a Fender Stratocaster. Instead it features another venerable rock-and-roll instrument, the semi-acoustic, accompanied by more human percussion courtesy of the hands and feet. The Stratocaster's many associations flow through the song – symbolic of a whole youth culture, they are myriad – and its sound and look are woven around them, mutually dependent; two minutes and fifty-one seconds that define an era and then send echoes on into the present day and towards the future. Jonathan's version of 'Blue Moon' is the first of the two surviving songs featuring Curly and Ron Wilson. Possibly featuring Jonathan's best-ever recorded guitar work, with its soft R&B feel it glides along on a velvet rhythm cushion. Its companion piece, the instrumental 'Sleepwalk', has a similar languid charm and instrumental prowess, conjuring up slow motion on a moonlit night. Brennan explains how it came to be there. 'A hit in the late fifties for a duo named Santo and Johnny . . . That was one of the instrumentals everybody learned, slow-dance instrumentals, sort of part of the fabric of our life. We had played it on stage a couple of times but not like that! He just started playing it . . . everybody loved that song.' Charles Trenet's 'Que Reste-t-il de Nos Amours?', with its solitary semi-acoustic guitar accompanying the reliving of a lost love, is reminiscent of 'I Hear You Calling Me' and completes a trilogy, with 'Miracles Will Start to Happen' and 'Sleepwalk', of songs concerning the power of the mind and the spirit over the body and the earthbound.

After the release of *Jonathan Richman* Jonathan wrote a four-page 'biography' of his career, an account of his 'First Twenty Years in Show Business' which was sent out to subscribers to his mailing list. From his childhood to the present day, it is a fascinating account of the development of his musical ideas, all told with self-deprecatory humour and many examples of his ability to pinpoint events.

At the beginning of 1990 an interview appeared in *Billboard* magazine which confirmed the evidence of his recent live shows and the *Jonathan Richman* album: 'I'm more or less formally announcing my career as a solo artist. I can't say forever, but I have no plans to do anything else.'

A surprise disclosure in Jonathan's résumé had been the news that he was working on a country record – particularly surprising as it was also to feature a host of specialist musicians hired for this one-off project. Although his love for this kind of music had begun with his association with Gram Parsons in the summer of 1973, it had never really surfaced in his work before, and a whole album in this vein was an unusual step to take.

Recorded in Springfield, Missouri, *Jonathan Goes Country* featured an experienced country crew of backing musicians and technicians. Despite that, it is in no way a mainstream country album but more like a collision between that and a rock-and-roll album – Jonathan shows plenty of respect for his musicians and their background, but this is never allowed to get in the way of something that must remain definably his. His vocals and guitar-playing remain resolutely in his own style and, although some of the songs are already familiar, their restyling is in no sense a dilution of their essential Richman qualities. The result is an intriguing and deeply satisfying blend but one that was not to be given the kind of financial backing that could have made it more than a purely artistic success, an outcome that Andy Paley thinks was entirely impossible. 'I think Jonathan had a chance to maybe go somewhere in the country charts. There's a big misconception about country music . . . Everybody buys country records; they're the biggest thing in the world right now . . . I just don't understand why they didn't push it, because it was a great job he did on that record . . . I know these guys. They didn't mess around; it was very professionally done.'

Highlights here include an instrumental interpretation of Tammy Wynette's 'Your Good Girl's Gonna Go Bad' (which features Jonathan and co-producer D. Clinton Thompson trading rock-and-roll and country solos) and 'You're Crazy for Taking the Bus', which takes the slowest, most uncomfortable but also the most fascinating form of transport through California (and onward), encountering plenty of examples of variety as the spice of life on the way. There is also a version here of Ronee Blakely's 'Rodeo Wind', the perfect choice with its comparisons of rodeo and rock and roll and its observations that are so near to those of Jonathan's own songs. Although the album would lead to the filming of Jonathan's first-ever video, for 'Since She Started to Ride', there was not enough money around to tour it abroad properly or to promote it in other ways. What it is, though, is an album made entirely as Jonathan wanted it made – on his terms, then, a complete success.

Touring in Europe again in August 1990 Jonathan was now playing solo acoustic shows once more, often very lengthy ones – and this was no mean feat without a band behind him. Despite the absence of literal electricity, there was no lack of the metaphorical kind – the sole accompaniment of an acoustic guitar was enough to provide plenty of quintessential rock and roll, including lead breaks of wonderful invention and variation. In November Jonathan went to Japan for the first time, where he was overjoyed at the emotional response of an audience unable to rely on a detailed understanding of his lyrics, then on to Australia before a return to the USA.

The live tracks that turn up on *Having a Party with Jonathan Richman* were recorded at gigs in the USA throughout 1991. The album was produced at John Girton's studio in Grass Valley by Brennan. Once again, though, a handful of cuts was all that would finally remain of a project that had once seemed almost complete, as Brennan recounts: 'We recorded that entire album live, and pretty much had it completed, and Jonathan again walked out of the studio and began playing it in the car, and we turned on the machines and started over again – he doesn't like old stuff. Two tracks were recorded in Milwaukee, the rest in Madison – it was good stuff, too. I was happy for what he did in the studio, but, conversely, I'm sorry he didn't get to do an entire live record.'

After the one-off country album, Jonathan returned on this album to the 'solo' recording experiments of *Jonathan Richman*, and the use of live material was an attempt to get even closer to the intimacy of his public performances. *Having a Party with Jonathan Richman* features four songs recorded live with Jonathan alone on stage and nine more were recorded in the studio – perhaps surprisingly this mix makes a very coherent whole.

Among the highlights is 'My Career as a Homewrecker', a plea for emotional honesty wrapped in a case history – Jonathan's youth – that lacks it. Some of the things he did to people were bad, but some of the people he hurt never told him, and that was bad, too. The final two verses are right on the edge, dangerous, as he acknowledges that the potential for these things is still inside him now. The mixture of emotional complexity and an honesty that lays him almost cruelly bare, set to music that is both yearning and powerful, makes this one of Jonathan's most poignant and powerful pieces of work. 'At Night' is another evocation of the unusual hours Jonathan keeps, depicting, in a way reminiscent of 'Lonely Financial Zone', nocturnal delights and inspirations in an alternative world of starlight, streetlight and moonlight, where 'The door to the arcane is thrust ajar'. The recited poem '1963' deals with memories of a period of time that cannot be recreated and Jonathan's attempts instead to recreate the feelings that time inspired, using a different stimulus. The result is a mixture of sadness and joy, given extra edge by the silence accompanying it. One of the live tracks here is 'Monologue About Bermuda', an extension of 'Down in Bermuda' that offers a perfect example of the pleasure Jonathan takes in stretching his songs into new shapes when he plays them on stage. The monologue, for which the song itself is temporarily suspended, is illustrated with musical references as Jonathan imitates the sound of the original Modern Lovers (after a fashion) and the local Bermuda Strollers, in order to show the new musical influences that were accompanying his change of attitudes back in 1973. This is more than just an explanation of the song; it is an extension of it, and this is something Jonathan does all the time in a live context. Improvisation is not really the right word; it is more the creation of a form of rock and roll entirely his own, one that can only really exist in the kind of intimate venues that he loves and where he continues to play.

There were two trips to Europe in 1991, the first in the spring and the second in the autumn, followed by more US dates. In between tours Jonathan had telephoned Moe Tucker with an intriguing suggestion, as she recalled when in London later that year. 'He asked how the record was going and he said: "Gee, I'd love to play on it, too, but I'm going to Europe." He came over here for a four- or five-week tour and then when he came back he called me and said: "Gee, I'd love to play rhythm guitar with you." So when I get home I'm going to ask him what he meant . . . I would love to have him play . . . '

On the UK leg of the spring European tour Jonathan was supported by the Rockingbirds, whose leader Alan Tyler had long been a fan, so much so that he wrote a fine Richman tribute, 'Jonathan, Jonathan', which they released as a single. The two acts shared an agency, and the Rockingbirds asked to support Jonathan during his trip to the UK. Two initial gigs went well and, although it was unusual for him to have a full band opening his shows on a tour, it was decided that, with both parties enjoying the arrangement, the Rockingbirds would continue on the bill for the duration. Alan Tyler remembers the experience. 'Jonathan travelled on his own, by train, and would stay in a hotel every night. Generally he would just turn up a little while before the gig. I think he made sure that he had a particular kind of microphone there, and he usually wouldn't need a soundcheck. We got to know that he didn't like any backline equipment on the stage, and we always cleared the gear off afterwards so he'd get a completely empty stage. It would just be him, his amplifier and his guitar, and he'd just walk out and get his sound straight away . . . We talked to him quite a lot . . . He told us a few stories about the Velvet Underground and Gram Parsons. He had lots and lots of stories . . . We were very impressed by his gymnastic displays in the dressing-room. On every occasion we'd share a dressing-room and, if there was space, he'd do all these exercises – loads of push-ups and handstands . . . He never had a rider, he wasn't interested in any riders at all . . . We'd try and clear the dressing-room out if it got too crowded; we were quite careful about not invading his space, but he was absolutely cool, he liked being round a rock-and-roll band.'

Jonathan returned to Europe in the spring, and again in the summer of 1992, and the Velvet Underground had obviously continued to occupy his thoughts in the meantime, as among the new material that he was featuring in his live set was a song written about them, their music and the impact that they had had on him.

The album from which new songs were being featured live – songs such as 'Parties in the USA', 'Velvet Underground', 'Rooming House on Venice Beach' and 'I Was Dancing in the Lesbian Bar' – was recorded in summer 1992, once again at John Girton's studio in Grass Valley. Compared to most of his recent albums *I, Jonathan* was to have a cast of thousands: with some of the musicians doubling up, there were effectively four singers, nine percussionists and drummers, four bass players and four guitarists. This record, then, came much closer to having a party with Jonathan than the album of that name, and Jonathan was later to say that he enjoyed making it more than he had any other.

*I, Jonathan* is an album of huge variety, both musically and lyrically, and one that was to gain almost universal critical acclaim. (Unfortunately Rounder had no British outlet for it, with the result that it had no proper release in the UK and was available only on import.) 'Parties in the USA', set to the riff of 'Hang On Sloopy' (and openly acknowledging it by quoting some of the lyrics), is a plea for innocent, unselfish fun at a time when it's in short supply. The song's mixture of moods – yearning, discontent, celebration – is mirrored in its changes of pace, which culminate in a hand-clapping, driving finale. 'Tandem Jump' relies almost exclusively on music for its effect: the lyrics do no more than set the scene for what is to be a face-to-face encounter with extremes of excitement and fear. Scared yells, the sound of an aeroplane door opening at 8,500 feet, a grinding, distorted punk riff, fast and dangerous lead breaks – reading about it, this could be a descent into a nightmare world. Listening to it, though, these dark motifs are beautifully subverted by humour and a very pure exhilaration, so that what is created is a bubbling cocktail of super-energized experiences. 'You Can't Talk to the Dude', kicked off by a growling, broody, slightly distorted electric guitar, is a bleak portrayal of stagnation and lack of sensitivity and the inevitable negative impact of these on a relationship. The combination of a minor key and an urgent rhythm propel the song forward with a melancholy beauty, entwining the sadness of its situation with optimism as to the eventual outcome.

'Velvet Underground' puts into song what Jonathan had been saying for years: that this band had a unique effect on him, one that
inspired him to start writing songs and making his own music. The
standard twelve-bar R&B format was probably the most important of
the Velvet Underground's points of musical departure, so it is an
appropriate one here, as well as making a suitable framework for the
verse from 'Sister Ray' that Jonathan includes. 'Sister Ray'! Why use
this, the most darkly decadent of Lou Reed's drug songs and musically a heaving, twisting rack of distortion, pulses and madness?
Maybe it was the song's honesty and unflinching self-expression, its
rhythm guitar core and its refusal to abandon a rock-and-roll heart
even at the very edge of its improvisation. (Incidentally, there's a
little lyrical variation that must come from Jonathan's own recollections of live Velvet Underground shows – the phrase 'busy licking up
her pusher's hand' that he quotes does not appear on the studio version of 'Sister Ray'.) Jonathan plays bass on 'Velvet Underground',
and it is the most primitive bassline that you will ever hear, echoing
the song's own observations on the benefits of simplicity. The Velvet
Underground, in applying invention and imagination to basic musical tools, aimed to heighten and project reality, not distort it, and that
is something that Jonathan has been doing ever since.

A song written by a man with 'lesbian bar' in the title could be
voyeuristic, it could be an attempt at political correctness, it could be
an anti-gay diatribe, but 'I Was Dancing in the Lesbian Bar' is none of
those things. For a start, it is much more a song about dancing than a
song about a lesbian bar – the setting is only relevant because of the
lack of inhibitions there that leads to open self-expression. There is a
certain *frisson*, of course, that comes from the association, but the
atmosphere here is one of refreshing disregard for convention side by
side with respect for other people. Musically it has a similar force to
'You Can't Talk to the Dude', propelled along by fat rhythm guitar,
this time at faster dancing speed and featuring the kind of soaring
lead/rhythm guitar break that, when played live, Jonathan would
deliver eyes wide, staring at the back of the hall, rapt at the huge rever-
berating sounds emerging from the speakers. 'Rooming House on

Venice Beach' returns to the territory of 'Those Conga Drums', Venice Beach in 1973. An ode to the kind of simplicity of living, in a sympathetic environment, that sweeps away the trappings of modernity and allows the past to seep back, this was another semi-improvised performance, allowing Jonathan to express his memories as they came into his mind. The backing musicians, none of whom had heard the song before, were given various percussion instruments, Jonathan made verses up on the spot, and the whole thing was recorded in one take. The result is a narrative set in a musical jungle and thriving there, with Jonathan inspired into producing a stream-of-consciousness recollection that, in turn, taps directly into the past. A new version of 'That Summer Feeling' allows the song to breathe, away from the 'arranged' sound of *Jonathan Sings!* There is also a new verse, a memory of a little girl (another recapturing of the past), sung with all the force of reliving the moment rather than just remembering it and almost overflowing with emotion as a result. Jonathan has always been trying to create this kind of magic in the studio and maybe once even thought it impossible – here he pulls it off on consecutive tracks. 'Grunion Run', an instrumental, is a raw take on the Ventures, aided by the newly nicknamed Ned 'Trem' Claflin. Perhaps not Jonathan's most inspired guitar performance, it nevertheless recreates the sound, via an authentic original melody, perfectly. 'A Higher Power', despite its celebratory up-tempo delivery and humour, is a reflective illustration of the power of love that transcends mortal capabilities, proving the existence of a superior entity. If Jonathan could be said to be religious, this is the form his religion takes: as free and open as the rest of his beliefs. The album's closing track, 'Twilight in Boston', is similarly reflective, but this time the pace is that of a slow walk through the area in which he grew up. Again improvised in the studio (as was 'Grunion Run'), here the music is like a backdrop in front of which a stream-of-consciousness evocation of a time and a place is pulled out of the ether. It is highlighted only briefly as Jonathan's acoustic guitar, accompanied by his own intakes of breath as he 'walks', illustrates the journey as a 'time for adventure'. Like musical Proust the past lives and breathes heightened, not lessened, by the passage of time.

In October 1992 Jonathan played a gig at New York's Lone Star Roadhouse at which he was reunited with Ellie Marshall and Beth Harrington – the first time the three of them had played together since 1984.

In the early nineties these Stateside gigs would be as frequent as ever, if not more so, but Jonathan now had a growing family to support (with Jenny now school-age and Jason in his teens) and, with the problem of transporting them over long distances, had decided to cut down on touring abroad. Europe, which had become used to visits at least once a year and often more often, would now have to be content with rarer sightings of Jonathan.

Also around this time Creation Records in the UK had started a programme of reissues of his Beserkley material on their Rev-Ola label. With the release, too, of *Live at the Longbranch Saloon*, the first proper document of the original Modern Lovers on stage, Jonathan's low profile of recent years was gradually being raised.

In February 1993 Jonathan was interviewed in *Spin* magazine, listing his current listening (including Nolan Strong and the Diablos, Sam Cooke and Maurice Chevalier), describing his ideal holiday (sleeping bags in the Mojave desert) and charmingly deflecting the shameless romantic advances of the interviewer Julia Sweeney of *Saturday Night Live* fame.

In May Tom Hibbert of *Q* magazine approached Jonathan in Boston, armed with questions about the original Modern Lovers, lunacy, the meaning of certain lines in his songs and the state of his finances. He did not get on too well this time but later, at a gig at the Point in Atlanta, he found a 'glorious charm' in Jonathan's songs and saw 'a topping humorist and a really fabulous entertainer to boot'. All of which goes to show that it does not what preconceptions people may have about Jonathan as long as they can see him perform his songs – that is when they really make up their minds.

Also in May, Luke Haines, of the highly rated English band the Auteurs, appeared in *Melody Maker*'s 'Rebellious Jukebox' feature where artists discuss the songs that have had the biggest impact on them. Number three on his list was 'Roadrunner', which he described as 'the best record ever made by the best group ever.' In a year when Jonathan's song-writing had also been praised by Teenage Fanclub, a new generation of influential admirers was emerging.

On 16 September Jonathan could be seen on US network television, appearing during the first week of the *Conan O'Brien Show* (successor to the long-running and hugely successful *David Letterman Show*). Jonathan chatted, performed a new song, 'Vampire Girl', and was relaxed and funny. He made the first of what would be many return appearances shortly afterwards, on 5 November, this time with Julia Sweeney. They performed a song specially written by Jonathan for the occasion, 'Just Because I'm Irish'. (Later Jonathan would film a cameo with Julia for the movie *It's Pat* – but real success on the large screen would have to wait a while longer.)

'Vampire Girl' is a bewitching comic tale of a female Goth whose sinister aspect intrigues Jonathan and then charms him in a pay-off that reveals that she has all of his records. A short story in a Chuck Berry musical setting with a spooky middle-eight, a hint of the perverse and a double helping of curiosity added to the brew.

Another song that Jonathan started performing around this time is the similarly lucid and fluent 'Let Her Go into the Darkness'. Here, though, the humour is further down in the mix, and the result is a piece of work with the complexity of 'My Career as a Homewrecker' and 'You Can't Talk to the Dude', the moral of which is immediately apparent from the title. For Jonathan to espouse a journey into darkness seems to be to turn his world upside down, but it is not advice for himself: it is directed at a boyfriend whose ex-girlfriend has decided on that course anyway. As in 'You Can't Talk to the Dude' truth and hope must be given room to breathe; the truth is that nothing can stop her and the hope is that she will emerge the other side wiser for the experience. A minor key, three chords and rhythm guitar breaks between the verses that understand and live out the emotion at the song's heart create a simple setting capable of supporting this most complex set of emotions.

Although Jonathan was enjoying his new-found television fame, what he was concentrating on at the time of these appearances was another new album, recorded between the two shows. Neither 'Vampire Girl' nor 'Let Her Go into the Darkness' were to appear on it, however, as *¡Jonathan, Te Vas a Emocionar!* (Jonathan, you're getting all emotional) is a collection of Richman standards, two Mexican songs and two instrumentals with, as the title suggests, all the lyrics in Spanish. No new self-penned songs feature here. The reason for this is that nothing was to be allowed to distract attention from the language of the album – and the room this would give for a whole new expression of emotion. Despite a form even more unusual than the *Jonathan Goes Country*, this is still very much a Jonathan Richman album – his own songs are not embellished with artificial devices in order to translate them musically as well as lyrically. The instrumentation is as sparse as ever: six out of the fifteen tracks feature Jonathan backed only by his own acoustic guitar with augmentation of the songs limited to unobtrusive congas/bongos and piano and guitar fills.

'The Neighbors' and 'Cerca' each receive their third outing on a Richman album and, like the songs making their second appearance, are little changed in arrangement from the original versions. All this clears away anything that could have interfered with the essence of this project: this is raw Richman expressed through and immersed in Spanish culture. Brennan, producing again, relished the experience. 'That was a great record to make – [different from] the others. With the others there was a certain familiar quality because we used a lot of the same people and we'd learned to work in certain ways . . . I don't speak a word of Spanish, none of the musicians on the record spoke any Spanish, so we had no idea what he was singing and he was somewhat in character for a lot of that because he would be speaking to us over the talkback in the studio in Spanish and we'd be nodding our heads and saying: "Yes, absolutely."'

In her liner notes Lydia Ledesma, who helped translate Jonathan's lyrics, comments that he has managed in his study of Spanish to understand not just the language but also the culture and the emotions at its heart, so the words of his songs and the passion behind them flow easily from English into Spanish. The translations are free, the priority being expression of a song's heart rather than a literal transfer of meaning. Sometimes this results in striking differences: 'You Can't Talk to the Dude' becomes 'No Te Oye' (He's not listening to you), and the references to the Fenway and Kenmore in the first verse of 'Now Is Better Than Before' become, on 'Ahora Es Mejor', a dread of 'A stale monotony/Where before there was fire'. In his own liner notes Jonathan identifies an early special empathy with Spanish audiences in his career and a desire to communicate with them on their own terms. To have achieved this puts him on a new emotional plateau; always searching for fulfilling ways to convey his feelings, here he finds a unique opportunity.

The six tracks backed solely by Jonathan's acoustic guitar are straightforward renderings, stripping the songs down to their basics and allowing the Spanish language to bring them their new life unhindered. Jonathan enjoys giving fresh expression to these familiar songs and he pours his feelings into the consonant sounds, relishing the emphasis at the end of words that in English would come one syllable earlier.

Elsewhere on the album, 'Pantomima de "El Amor Brujo"' ('Love the Magician') by Manuel de Falla, the early-twentieth-century composer of ballets and theatrical pieces, is an instrumental duet on acoustic guitars by Jonathan and Brennan. This is Jonathan's most formal musical outing yet. The piece is divided into the 'acts' of a 'pantomima' and is a graceful and respectful account of the breakdown of love. 'Los Vecinos' is shorter than 'The Neighbors' (of which it is a version), compacting its message but retaining the alternating male/female vocal line courtesy of Ivy Ledesma who, Brennan says, 'was just a sweetheart. She'd never been on a record before in this country. Jonathan flew her in just to do that one song and she just came in and belted it out – she was great on first take.' 'Compadrito Corazón' ('My Heart, My Best Friend') by Manuel Esperon and Jesus Camacho, a Mexican song with Jonathan's guitar embellished by that of John Girton, is a plea for a disillusioned lover not to lose faith in love. Its original ending recommending alcohol as a way of forgetting despair is replaced by Jonathan with a new couplet urging acceptance and then, through that, transcendence.

With minimal publicity (and again only import availability in the UK), a Spanish-language album was never likely to stand much chance of making a commercial impact on the US and UK markets, and unfortunately it is likely to remain, despite its many merits and singularity, one of Jonathan's least-known projects.

By the time Jonathan recorded *¡Jonathan, Te Vas a Emocionar!* the Red Hot Organization had released the third in a line of AIDS awareness productions, *No Alternative*. Jonathan had been asked whether he had anything available for inclusion and contributed a live version of 'I Love Hot Nights' recorded in Milwaukee in 1991 at the same time as the live material on *Having a Party with Jonathan Richman*. For most artists, coming up with an out-take or a live version of a song would present few problems as these things tend nowadays to be stored and archived for a variety of potential future uses. For Jonathan, however, when something is finished it is finished and it is time to move on – all of his recordings, studio and live, have a shelf-life of a year. After that they are destroyed. This is a process that Brennan only became reconciled to with considerable difficulty. 'It's like a painting; you don't go back twenty-five years later . . . I've never heard of anybody doing that. The first time he told me to dispose of a tape I was stunned . . . Red Hot were looking for something unreleased and the year wasn't up on a live tape I had done for him . . . I managed to retrieve one song . . . another two weeks and we would have had nothing.'

As well as re-releasing *Beserkley Chartbusters* on CD in 1993 Rev-Ola had also reissued Moe Tucker's album *Life in Exile After Abdication*. This reissue, as well as having some unmissable extra tracks from an earlier EP, has new sleeve notes from Jonathan. In them he relives his excitement on first hearing the Velvet Underground and describes Moe's part in the creation of their sound, through her unique approach and technique. He talks, too, about his love of the raw feel of her recent recordings and his continuing affection for her.

Before long, there would be further poignant reasons to remember the Velvet Underground.

# 10 I'M SO CONFUSED

O N 6 May 1994 Jonathan, back in England for the first time in two years, played Upstairs at the Garage in Islington, London. Whoever booked this tiny venue must have regretted it. His two-year absence, far from allowing people to forget about Jonathan, seemed, if anything, to have made their hearts grow fonder, and many had to be turned away from the packed hall. Of those who made it inside only a lucky few at the front had a good view, and a few insistent hecklers at the back became a minor annoyance for Jonathan. The evening, though, after a couple of tense moments, was finally a triumph. Songs included a version of Tom Waits' 'The Heart of Saturday Night' (now a regular part of his set), a rather good Elvis impression and a new song, 'I'm Not Afraid to Reveal', about the need to conquer fear of expressing emotion. For those not at the front Jonathan, who was barely discernible anyway, would, during instrumental breaks, disappear completely. If those people could have fought their way forwards to see the stage the mystery would have been solved: he had three different microphones – one each for vocal and acoustic guitar centre-stage and a third, stage-left, at knee height. This third microphone would come into use when Jonathan, inspired to produce some solo guitar work, would leave the first two and, guitar in hand, stride a couple of yards across the stage, where he would continue playing on bended knee. This sight would also have explained the unaccountable tone and volume changes in the middle of songs – the gap between the pick-up ranges of the two different guitar microphones. This was a typical Jonathan manoeuvre – only he would consider such an option to get round the impossibility of 'switching' from rhythm to lead on an acoustic guitar. It was pretty daring by conventional standards and another 'neo-Brechtian' device for grabbing the attention of the audience.

The next night Jonathan played the Grand in Clapham, south London. 'Fender Stratocaster' had new verses of rock-and-roll history, while another new song, 'Wait for Her', discussed Jonathan's long estrangement from Gail in the seventies. 'Pablo Picasso' set the scene for its own inspiration – a bench on the New York subway where someone had left a life story of the painter, and the version of 'Back in Your Life' that Jonathan went on to play was a now epic account of his attempts to woo Gail, with narrative outweighing verse.

Although a much larger venue than that of the night before, the Grand was packed. The upper tier of the circle had initially been left closed, but such was the weight of numbers outside waiting patiently in pouring rain to get in that it was opened up and immediately filled. Despite minimal publicity and no proper release for his current album, Jonathan showed himself to be still a very potent live draw.

While in the UK this time Jonathan appeared on Jools Holland's influential BBC television programme, *Later* (introduced as 'Sir Jonathan Richman'). He only performed one song, 'Now Is Better Than Before' (apart from joining in the traditional opening jam with the other artists appearing on the show), but it was a striking performance. Once again it featured a guitar solo on bended knee, Jonathan's amplification arrangement the same here as for his concert performances. When the programme ended, the closing credits featured a shot of him in freeze-frame.

Also appearing on this edition of *Later* was Evan Dando of the Lemonheads. Dando, a fellow Bostonian, had been interviewed in the August edition of *Vox* magazine and had spoken about meeting Jonathan who had given him a list of ten points to bear in mind when being interviewed. Dando said that he could 'identify with Jonathan a lot' and that the original Modern Lovers were, along with the Velvet Underground and the Stooges, his favourite band.

More gigs followed when Jonathan returned to the USA in the autumn (in October he shared a bill in Wisconsin with Moe Tucker and Sterling Morrison). He was also awarded the accolade of a brass star at the Boston branch of Tower Records for his contribution to 'the Boston Sound' (at the ceremony he played 'Fender Stratocaster'), and a party was attended by friends, family and various music business representatives.

In January 1995 Ian Broudie of the Lightning Seeds talked about 'the songs that make him shiver' in *Melody Maker*'s 'Rebellious Jukebox' series. Included was *Jonathan Richman and the Modern Lovers*, and Jonathan was described as 'one of the most underrated performers around. I could have chosen almost anything by him.'

A few months earlier Soolimon Rogie, whose music Jonathan so loved, had died and on 15 January Jonathan phoned Brennan to give him news of another tragic loss, that of Ted Hawkins, another of their favourite artists and someone with whom they had loved working. After spending many years performing on the boardwalk in Venice, California, Hawkins had finally been 'discovered', after which he had recorded an album, *Watch Your Step*, for Jonathan's label, Rounder. Despite going on to greater success, he had continued to play on the boardwalk. While playing a week's worth of shows in 1987 at a beach-front club in Southern California called Safari Sam's, Jonathan had been asked to choose a different support act each night. He had chosen Ted Hawkins for every night. Brennan remembers these shows as 'a real magical time'.

In the autumn of 1994 Jonathan had recorded an album, *You Must Ask the Heart*, which was eventually released in May 1995. It features most of the new songs he had been performing live in recent months. Studio time for this album was longer than normal (eleven days) but not as intensive: six-hour stints during the daytime, four-hour ones at night. The personnel was a familiar crew of John Girton, this time on guitar and saxophone, Ned Claflin, now playing keyboards, Jim

Washburn on bass, Joseph Marc on piano, Scot Woodland on congas and backing vocals from the Baltimores.

Overall, the songs here are mid-tempo with a kind of lounge-bar feel conveyed by organ, piano and low-key percussion, punctuated by bursts of up-tempo rock and roll. There is a smoother finish than on 1993's *I, Jonathan* but a similar range of material and a number of musical surprises contributing a similarly satisfying whole. As usual, the running order was carefully worked out, balancing mid- and up-tempo, with an early burst of rock and roll giving way to love songs and then an unaccompanied double finale.

Of the stand-out tracks, 'To Hide a Little Thought' is a tightly thought-out and presented exposition of Jonathan's desire never to lie – an integral part of his make-up that Brennan has observed at close hand. 'He lives his life in public. He's the same guy when he's out admiring his garden as he is when he's painting, and he's the same guy when he's painting as he is plugging into a Fender Twin on stage. Rule One is "Never lie", ever, under any circumstances, and sometimes that can be painful, but I have never heard an untruth come out of that guy.' For Jonathan, however, the refusal to lie is not only a moral stance but also a way of producing excitement from con-frontation: lying, on the contrary, even when well intentioned, makes him 'lifeless'.

Tom Waits's 'The Heart of Saturday Night' is cranked up and sobered up ('barrelling' rather than 'stumbling' down the boulevard) and as a result unexpectedly fits neatly the Richman recipe for the kind of good time that slips indefinably into what seems to be another dimension. The tempo is emphasized by a frantic electric rhythm guitar backing (his only use of the electric instrument on the whole album) and the song receives a final flourish reminiscent of the original Modern Lovers' 'Ride Down on the Highway'. 'That's How I Feel' is an elemental stream of pure rock and roll featuring some of the finest, most intense rhythm-guitar-playing you could wish to hear – and it is played on an acoustic; Brennan compares Jonathan here to 'some manic banjo player from vaudeville'. The guitar is backed by repeated, sustained organ chords, bass and drums and provides a hugely energetic and inspired rhythm solo before fading out in full flow. Amanda McBroom's 'The Rose' was originally popularized in the eponymous Bette Midler film and seems an unlikely choice for a Jonathan Richman album; Brennan initially tried to dissuade him from using it. However, after an initial run-through backed only by his own guitar there was, Brennan says, obviously 'something in the song that touched him' and it stayed. Familiar it may be, but, in essence, its simplicity, its message of love overcoming fear and its disciplined but developed melody make it the perfect choice for a cover version by Jonathan. 'Walter Johnson' is a straightforward reappraisal of the track from *Rockin' and Romance*. The earlier version had been backed only by acoustic guitar, but this one removes even this last layer of clothing so that the song stands naked, its evocation of purity now completely pure itself.

For Jonathan's next album, Brennan would hand the producer's baton back to his old friend Andy Paley. For him, though, working with Jonathan is 'unlike any other experience I have ever had . . . He is just a dreamboat to work with. Mr Richman has a persistence of vision that never ceases to amaze me . . . I'm a very fortunate guy.'

By now Jonathan had also recorded an old Egyptian folk song called 'Mustapha' for a French label. For this project Brennan had an Egyptian drum sent down from a mail-order catalogue and Jonathan, of course, had no problem finding an Egyptian-born drummer who just happened to be running a local convenience store. The drummer went into the studio with the drum and, for a nominal fee, recorded the song in two takes.

Despite the generally upbeat tone, the recording of *You Must Ask the Heart* had taken place against the most poignant emotional backdrop of Jonathan's life: the ongoing breakdown of his relationship with Gail, his partner of seventeen years and muse for even longer. It would be no exaggeration to say that she had been the foundation of his life. The effect of this upon Jonathan does not need to be spelled out and can be seen most clearly in his work where, as always, he would portray his life with unflinching honesty. Suffice to say, it is impossible to underestimate.

In late summer came yet more sad news about another of Jonathan's musical heroes. On 30 August 1995 Sterling Morrison died at his home in Poughkeepsie, New York, of a lymphoma, cancer of the lymph glands. Not only was Sterling guitarist with the Velvet Underground and as such a profound musical influence on Jonathan, he was also one of his oldest friends and had kept in regular contact with him over the years. Jonathan would write to him when on tour, lend him books and suggest where he should buy his clothes; there had also been talk of possible musical collaboration in the future. Sterling thought of Jonathan as 'a real good friend'. He was certainly that to Jonathan.

In July Jonathan had played two sets at New York's Knitting Factory. Not surprisingly, considering the turmoil in his emotional life at the time, the first set had been subdued, but the second set was upbeat and full of life, indicative of a desire on his part to overcome sadness and emerge the other side, a desire that would become even more evident over the next months.

Understandably there was to be no European tour in 1995, but if US gigs in October and November saw Jonathan occasionally sad (singing 'The Rose' live sometimes because it made him feel better) they also saw him mostly happy, the joy in his songs reflecting back on to himself from his audiences. At the Lounge Ax in Chicago the after-show crowd dispersed relatively quickly, leaving the bar almost empty, but those who stayed were treated to the sight of Jonathan dancing to the music from the jukebox. In Northampton, Massachusetts, a little girl's request led to an improvised song; in Minneapolis Jonathan briefly played bass with the opening band. Backing Jonathan at this stage was a new drummer, Tommy Larkins; and accompanying him to gigs sometimes was his daughter Jenny, for whom a new song, 'My Little Girl's Got a Full-Time Daddy Now', had been written.

Jonathan had been using pick-up drummers for a while now as he toured around different parts of the USA – a simple rhythm accompaniment without having to worry about tuning or key changes was what he was after – but Tommy had stuck. On their first appearance together Tommy set up his kick-drum and snare, Jonathan arrived and said: 'I bet you're the drummer', and off they went. The two of them hit it off straight away and it was the start of a relationship that is still going strong. Tommy had not been that familiar with Jonathan's material to start with, although he had seen him play, but that meant he brought few preconceptions to the job. This, together with a natural feeling for rhythm and the ability to play a backbeat no matter what was happening on the stage in front of him, meant that he had all the qualifications. Tight enough to keep the songs together, loose enough to adapt instantly to Jonathan's changes of direction within and between songs (he says he loves it when Jonathan plays something he has never heard before), Tommy also gives him more room to breathe, allowing him the freedom of not always having to keep the rhythm of the song going on his own. Although within a year Tommy would be joined by a keyboard player and bassist in Jonathan's new band, this would be strictly a short-term project – Tommy is all the accompaniment Jonathan really needs.

On 19 October Jonathan and Tommy played at the Middle East Café in Cambridge, Massachusetts. 'My Little Girl's Got a Full-Time Daddy Now' was played here, and it deals directly and characteristically openly with Jonathan's break-up with Gail. It is an uplifting song, though, tearing hope and satisfaction from despair as he proudly enjoys the development in his relationship with his daughter. The beat is insistent and Jonathan's delivery urgent, as if the words must be forced out and then forced into the tempo to convey the message with enough passion. At the end the pace slows dramatically, with guitar arpeggios and washes of cymbal drawing it to a gentle close. Here, in the heart of New England, Jonathan jokes about trying to ensure that all the people he knows are on the guest list (difficult when there are 'about four thousand' of them) and outlines his position as an expatriate Bostonian 'exploring Californian culture and . . . report[ing] back a thing or two'. 'Velvet Underground', too, gets a hometown introduction, as Jonathan remembers seeing the band 'about sixty times at the Boston Tea Party down there at 53 Berkeley

Street . . . We know . . . the Velvet Underground played here many times because there is archaeological, fossilitic record! And I was there to prove it!' Jonathan's extended quote here from 'Sister Ray' is soaked in distortion which carries on into his solo and then continues to be a feature throughout the night, used sparingly and intensely as a channel for the expression of his loneliness. There are reflections here of course of the original Modern Lovers, and it is almost as if he is remembering how he used to deal with his feelings of isolation during that era and is now repeating the process. Jonathan's loss is part of his life and therefore becomes part of the live performances that he gives. However, in this show and the ones to follow, it is obvious that, even though she is physically apart from him, he feels Gail's presence still to be with him through the experiences and the love that they have shared. Accordingly, therefore, he still plays the songs that he wrote about her (at this gig, 'The Girl Stands Up to Me Now' and 'Everyday Clothes').

'Not Just a "Plus One" on the Guest List Anymore' (introduced as a 'brand-new one . . . in fact I barely know it myself') may be an explicit account of the end of a relationship and mix minor chords with its major ones, but it is up-tempo and looks to the future. What is really extraordinary, though, is that it is Gail's future and is written entirely from her point of view (the only mention of Jonathan is 'without me'). There is a complete absence of bitterness here and instead there is a joy in the search for happiness of someone he loves. It is hard to think of anyone else who could so invert the customary pattern of the break-up of a relationship as to see selfless optimism rather than self-pity or anger. The version of 'Let Her Go into the Darkness' following this was introduced by long repetition of thick guitar chords, then lifted by a reggae lilt and finally pierced through the heart by a fuzz-laden guitar solo, lifting the pain out of the song, living it and then exorcizing it. It is almost as if the emotions purposely excluded from the previous song could be dealt with here anonymously. Jonathan would place these two songs together again in live shows. A stomping, fuzz-heavy 'Wipe Out' was followed by 'Fender Stratocaster', accompanied in part only by drum and clapping from the audience, and featuring an improvised verse about the 'summer wind buzzing' and how the Fender sound is 'thin . . . a kind of a lonely thing'.

In November Neil Young and Elliot Roberts announced the first signings to their new record label Vapor. Discussing these signings, Nick Kent wrote in the December issue of *Mojo* magazine: 'Most interesting of all, Young and his manager Elliot Roberts have signed one of the few rock iconoclasts perhaps even more bloody-minded than he is himself – Jonathan Richman.' With the seven album contract with Rounder fulfilled after *You Must Ask the Heart*, Jonathan had been approached earlier in the year by Vapor and a deal was now finally agreed. When he had originally signed with Rounder the label had been just right for him – willing to allow complete artistic freedom at a time when other labels would have been wary. Able there to express himself fully, he had produced some of his most satisfying work. Now, though, he was offered an opportunity to look to the future and go one better on a label with a higher profile. Vapor would give him the same licence but had more money available, making it better able to sustain his career – and, in Neil Young, it had a figurehead of unique integrity in the music business.

Almost immediately, a live album looked set for release but, with Jonathan excited about the new material he was writing – and the band he was putting together to play it – this was shelved in favour of a studio album, to be entitled *Surrender to Jonathan*.

On 1 and 2 May 1996 Jonathan, together with the new band, played two sell-out dates at London's neon-lit Jazz Café. The band consisted of Tommy Larkins on drums, Nick Augustine on bass and Dan Eisenberg on a Hammond organ that seemed to be held together purely by adhesive tape. The recruitment of Nick Augustine, a friend of Tommy's, had been pretty straightforward, but Jonathan had heard of Dan Eisenberg as a 'white kid who played in an all-black gospel church on Sunday mornings' and left a message on his answer machine. The message was an offer of a gig, paying $65. Dan was not all that impressed – until he realized, later on, that the message had been from Jonathan Richman.

In a way, just as Jonathan had gathered together the first Modern Lovers partly as a result of his loneliness, so, too, had he put together this similar formation (keyboards, bass and drums) at a time of similar isolation. It was almost as if the companionship of such a band would once again help to conquer those feelings.

The band gelled immediately they started playing together – which was just as well, because that was their first gig – and by the time they got to England they were performing at their peak.

On the second night at the Jazz Café, as Jonathan and the band, all three of whom would watch him intently throughout the set, made their way down to the stage from the upstairs dining area via a gallery and staircase, they were greeted by excited applause.

Jonathan, playing an electric/acoustic began the show in a green open-necked shirt with rolled-up sleeves, black trousers and loafers, only to return after a break in a blue-and-white-striped long-sleeved T-shirt for the second set. The change of clothing was appropriate because there were definitely two Jonathans performing – one sad, staring upwards and barely able on occasion to summon up enough vocal power to be heard, the other uplifted by the sound and feel of the music and by the love of the audience, energized and happy.

The opening song, 'Floatin'' (slightly different from the version that would appear on the album *Surrender to Jonathan*), was, in this form, really an exposition of Jonathan's state of mind on his first trip to Europe since his split with Gail and also a plea for understanding. Set to a two-chord rhythm similar to the one of 'That Summer Feeling', it describes his loss as it appeared to him in a dream and the way that, in real life, it brings the same disorientating sensation. His family are far away, not just in terms of distance but emotionally – and that is what makes their separation so hard to overcome. After this opening, with its opportunity to express his sadness and to try to dispel it, Jonathan's 'Welcome, everybody' was an invitation to lighten the mood. For the rest of the evening happiness would, more often than not, win out over sadness. Another new song, 'French Style', highlighting France's unique charm, was much more upbeat and set first to a reggae-ish lilt and then to a more driving beat with sustained organ chords. Dan Eisenberg's Hammond, with its sixties sound, would provide the ideal foil for Jonathan's guitar-playing throughout the show, but the two together could be an exotic combination as well when, as here, the music shifted away from traditional rock and roll. An organ riff was the instrumental hook for 'Just Look at Me', perhaps the catchiest of Jonathan's highly attractive batch of new songs. Many years ago, in 'Astral Plane', Jonathan had been convinced that physical proximity was not necessary to be truly with someone and, in an echo of that, he says what his earlier live shows had already shown – that there is so much joint history between him and Gail, and there are so many ways in which she has affected him and his life, that in reality she will always be with him. It was not just wishful thinking, he really believed it and, once again, could summon happiness from sadness in a transcendence the power of which cannot be undervalued. The firm conviction of the song and its performance was that love that had once existed will always exist. One of the evening's other new songs was 'Surrender', melodic but insistent, which argued at some length that love could only come after defences were dropped and the state of mind that saw a relationship as a struggle was rejected. Guitarless, gazing above the gallery, Jonathan let the band carry the music while he sang. For the final song the appreciative audience were silent for a version of Porter Wagoner's 'Satisfied Mind' that, with only the lightest of musical backing, allowed its words to seal the magic of the evening.

In July Jonathan and band were back in England for the four-day Phoenix Festival, before mixing more English dates with trips to Ireland, Scotland, Belgium, Sweden and Denmark.

On 9 August they played another sell-out date at London's Garage. Jonathan's last visit here had been to the tiny Upstairs room. This time, playing on the main stage, the venue was much more appropriate: larger capacity, bigger stage, better views. Jonathan was at the bar beforehand, getting a drink and modestly describing himself as 'with the band'. Not far away from him was a merchandise stand, which was well stocked with T-shirts, CDs, posters and a register on which to sign up for his mailing list – evidence that some effective commercial organization of his career was at last going on.

For this show, Jonathan (clad in blue-and-white Hawaiian shirt) had got himself a black Fender Telecaster, and the evening got off to a raw electric start with three instrumentals in one long power surge: 'Yo Jo Jo', 'Ecuadorian Folk Song' and an 'Egyptian Reggae' whose chopped Hammond organ was almost like an additional piece of percussion. 'Pablo Picasso', with its guitar/keyboard base, together with drum work from Tommy Larkins that was a near-perfect copy of the original, sounded almost as though it was being performed by the original Modern Lovers. Jonathan provided a fuzz/sustain solo to match, featuring short bursts of air-slicing distortion, and followed it with a coda that was like a spoken explanation, using the sounds of an electric guitar instead of words. Jonathan had been incorporating James Brown's 'Sex Machine' into his live shows for a while now, and tonight's version was a great work-out: pumping, grinding and churning, with fluid, popping basslines from Nick Augustine in the mid-song rhythm section spotlight. 'Vampire Girl' was accompanied by actions from Jonathan for the 'evil . . . scary' sections: two fingers pointing from the top of his head for horns, clenched fingers for claws and a long swoop behind him with his hand for a tail to complete the devilish picture. 'You Can't Talk to the Dude', with long guitar intro and finale, provided a frenetic end to the set proper. Jonathan, though, was presented with flowers and stayed to perform a cappella versions of 'Arrivederci Roma' and 'Sabor a Mí' as a final farewell.

A week after this Jonathan and band were back in England once more, supporting Pulp – at the special request of leader Jarvis Cocker – at day-long festivals in Chelmsford and Warrington. This appearance was followed a month later by the release of *Surrender to Jonathan* – a mixture of old songs reinterpreted, cover versions and some of the new songs that had recently been played live.

The album had been recorded in Los Angeles in a couple of studios – NRG and Your Place or Mine – and, although the budget was not huge by most standards, it allowed for the provision of session musicians such as the Vine Street Horns and accordionist Frank

Morroco to accompany Jonathan's band and regulars such as Ned Claflin and John Girton.

*Surrender to Jonathan* was produced by Andy Paley, and he says that right from the start the idea was to create variety without any preconceptions as to how any song would turn out. One shock for Andy was that Jonathan, keener than ever on putting his singing to the forefront, wanted to get someone else in to play all his guitar parts. Andy persuaded him that his was such a distinctive style that no one else would be able to successfully take over the role and, in the event, Jonathan would spend, if anything, more time than ever playing. He used, variously, an Ibanez jazz electric, a Gibson 335, a Telecaster and a Strat – not to mention a six-string bass. He also indulged his newly rediscovered love of distortion, as Andy recalls: 'Yeah, he got excited about that! Turn on a fuzz-tone, and he'd flip out. All of a sudden it would just wake him up.'

Most of the songs were recorded with Jonathan singing live and playing guitar at the same time, although on occasion, even in the middle of a take, Jonathan would stop playing guitar to concentrate on his vocals, but there was also some overdubbing which Jonathan was more than happy to undertake where appropriate.

The album that resulted from these sessions is undoubtedly Jonathan's most commercial since *Jonathan Sings!* As in his live performances of the time, there is an element of sadness, but it is one that is counterpointed by a positive affirmation of the happiness that he firmly believes will come out of it, brought out most strongly in some truly exuberant organ-, horn- and accordion-playing. Four songs on this album had previously been recorded by Jonathan, but the idea was to make them accessible to people who may not have heard them before – and, of course, to reinterpret them with the emphasis on the feeling behind the performance. Of these 'I Was Dancing in the Lesbian Bar' benefits from a particularly piercing fuzz solo, 'When She Kisses Me' emerges as a fully formed pop classic and 'Egyptian Reggae' becomes much more reggae than Egyptian. Most of these songs would already be familiar to Jonathan's fans, either from earlier albums or from recent live appearances. Of the latter, 'Satisfy' is a powerful up-front rock-and-roll song about the way only love can bring real satisfaction, and 'Floatin'' makes a fitting finale: an emotional album's most emotional song.

Jonathan's second video – for 'I Was Dancing in the Lesbian Bar' – was filmed to promote the album, and he seemed happy to undertake other promotional work as well, agreeing to several interviews, some more successful than others, and performing 'Surrender' (with the band) during another of his regular appearances on the *Conan O'Brien Show*.

Although there were US dates to celebrate the new album, by the time they had finished in November Jonathan and Tommy would once again be a duo. Using a full band this time had been purely a short-term undertaking. Having put out what he has described as a 'Technicolor' album – one that had helped him to pour vitality back into himself – and having drawn more strength from playing its material against a wide, supportive musical backdrop, it was time for Jonathan to return to what he still loved best. Life had become a little complicated – there had been four people to consider and plenty of hardware to transport – and it was time to simplify things again.

Both Tommy and Jonathan find it best to work as a duo. When on tour they can hire a car or a van, sit in the front, throw what little equipment there is in the back and concentrate on indulging their shared sense of humour and love of food.

In May 1997 Jonathan, as an admirer, interviewed John McCrea of 'easy listening' band Cake for *Interview* magazine, in which he had himself been interviewed back in 1973. As might be expected from someone with a not particularly high opinion of journalism, his piece was an unconventional one and seemed to involve nearly as many questions from McCrea to Jonathan as vice versa. More of a chat than an interview, it was refreshingly unpretentious and elicited the information from Jonathan that he was now trying to cut down from the roughly 110 shows he had played in the previous year.

In the middle months of 1997, in between tours, Jonathan took some time to pursue an unusual new interest for a singer: stonemasonry. He had already been an apprentice stonemason for a little while, enjoying the physicality of the work and the solidity of the achievements that resulted. He would later describe it as his 'third favourite thing in the world' (presumably behind music and painting).

Any chance there may have been, after his announced reduction in touring, of stonemasonry now becoming his favourite thing in the world disappeared, however, towards the end of the year. Jonathan was contacted by the Farrelly Brothers of *Dumb and Dumber* fame and asked to come up with some music for their new film *There's Something About Mary*.

Nearly two years earlier Jonathan had appeared in the Farrellys' previous film, *Kingpin*, singing two of his own songs in the background of a bar scene. Having been fans of his for some years, the brothers had sent Jonathan a film script to look at; despite not having at that stage known their work, and having had offers before that he had rejected, he had read the script – and liked it. For this next project, though, his credits would see him as much more than just 'Tavern Band Member'. Jonathan cut short his end-of-year tour as well as shelving a proposed visit to Europe in 1998 to travel down to Miami where filming was to take place.

In Miami with Tommy Jonathan proceeded not only to record three songs for the soundtrack but to compose the film's incidental music: watching rushes of the film Jonathan would get ideas and then go over to Peter Farrelly's house where they would be rubber-stamped. With no real budget constraints, Los Angeles-based session men were brought in to the ensuing recording when needed, and plenty of exotic percussion was added. This was a new experience for Jonathan, allowing him as it did to experiment across a whole range of new musical ideas – and he enjoyed it to the full. The atmosphere during the making of the film was laid back and very 'anti-Hollywood', almost like being in the middle of an extended family. It turned out, moreover, that Jonathan was to be asked not only to write the music but also to appear in the film. He and Tommy were to play a pair of wandering minstrels, much as Nat King Cole and Stubby Kaye had done in *Cat Ballou*. To start with, this proposal had been presented as merely an idea that might not work, and there had been no guarantees that their scenes would not end up on the cutting-room floor. The Farrellys, however, liked them – and so did preview audiences.

After two and a half months in Miami the project was complete. While they waited for the film to appear in cinemas, Jonathan and Tommy were already looking forward to their next challenge: the recording of a new album.

Entitled *I'm So Confused*, this was recorded at New York's Electric Ladyland and produced by former Cars leader and old Boston associate Ric Ocasek. The recording, beginning on 5 May, took three weeks, during which time Ocasek added plenty of his own synthesizer to a selection of mainly new songs that also included new versions of 'Affection' and 'When I Dance'.

While in New York Jonathan had been invited to play at Joey Ramone's Coney Island High birthday bash on 18 May (incidentally, in Jim Bessman's book *Ramones: An American Band* Jonathan is acknowledged as 'the first person to ever *dance* to the Ramones'). Here he surprised and delighted everyone not only by playing 'Girlfriend' and an extremely rare 'Roadrunner' but also by appearing with Ernie Brooks for the first time since 1975. Ernie had mentioned that he would be free should Jonathan feel a bass player was appropriate to the occasion, and Jonathan had accepted the offer.

Meanwhile, back in England, Tjinder Singh of Cornershop (who had covered Jonathan's 'Angels Watching Over Me') was interviewed in *Record Collector* magazine. He described the band's recent UK number one single, *Brimful of Asha*, as 'pure Jonathan Richman'.

By July advance showings in the USA of *There's Something About Mary* were being received with enthusiasm. Whereas the Farrellys' previous work had often not gone down well with women, it seemed that this one was scoring equally highly with both sexes. Reviews, when they started to appear, were generally favourable; several mentioned Jonathan appreciatively and there were articles about him in the *Village Voice*, *Entertainment Weekly* and *USA Today*, not to mention *Rolling Stone* where he was photographed with the film's star Cameron Diaz at the première. Jonathan would also make US network television appearances to publicize the film: on the *Howie*

*Mandel Show* with the rest of the cast and on the *Conan O'Brien Show* – where Conan was glad to congratulate such a long-time regular of the show on his success. On both occasions Jonathan sang the theme song to the film.

By the beginning of August *There's Something About Mary* was number three in the US box-office charts and taking $24 million a week in receipts – and Jonathan could be seen in over two thousand cinemas across the USA. In September it would reach the number one slot.

On 6 August Jonathan began a short tour with sell-out dates at New York's Knitting Factory. Three more shows in Cambridge from the 10th to the 12th were also all sold out, and the *Boston Globe* featured one in a long, positive review. The *Chicago Tribune* published an even longer profile-cum-interview, and the *SF Weekly*, a San Francisco alternative newspaper, made him their cover star with a five-page in-depth career review and interview inside.

In September Jonathan made a guest appearance on an edition of *Saturday Night Live* hosted by Cameron Diaz, and a month later Jonathan's new album, *I'm So Confused*, was released, its material as rich as ever, its sound sharp and focused, with Ric Ocasek's understated synthesizers bringing splashes of colour to the reflections on love and melancholy summed up by the album's title. In the same month Jonathan and Tommy played at Neil Young's annual benefit for the Bridge School, a special school for children with severe speech and physical ailments, alongside Young himself and REM, and received a standing ovation.

Jonathan, who grew up feeling totally alone, who threw away success not just once but twice when it proved to be the wrong kind and then resolutely refused to compromise his art with the remotest artifice, seems finally to have been given recognition for the purity of his vision and the way he expresses it.

It could even be said that Jonathan is now famous and, if so, no one has deserved it more – and no one will know better what to do with it.

# INTERVIEW SOURCES

**Page**

16   Kristine McKenna, *New York Rocker*, June 1982

32   Nick Kent, *New Musical Express*, 20 May 1978

42   Scott Cohen, *Interview*, August 1973

61   Judy Nylon, *New Musical Express*, 20 September 1975

117   Nick Kent, ibid.

128   Kristine McKenna, ibid.

131   Geoffrey Himes, *Washington Post*, 10 February 1981

135   George Parsons, *Option*, May 1983

151   Bruce Dessau, *Blitz*, May 1986

168   Julia Sweeney, *Spin*, February 1993

168   Tom Hibbert, *Q*, May 1993

174–5   Evan Dando, *Vox*, August 1994

188   Tjinder Singh, *Record Collector*, May 1998

# SELECT DISCOGRAPHY

In order to keep the discography simple, each album and single has been mentioned only once – unless different versions are particularly noteworthy. Entries, therefore, only apply to original releases. Where these have occurred simultaneously in the USA and the UK, the US version has been listed.

**ALBUMS** MODERN LOVERS

*The Modern Lovers*; Home of the Hits, HH 1019 (USA, 1976).

*The Original Modern Lovers*; Bomp, BLP 4021 (USA, 1981).

*The Modern Lovers*; Rhino, RDTLP 70091 (USA, 1986). A re-release with extra tracks, sleeve notes and photographs.

*Live at the Long Branch Saloon*; Fan Club, 422439 (France, 1992).

*Precice Modern Lovers Order*; Rounder, ROUN 9042 (USA, 1994). A USA-only release of *Live at the Long Branch Saloon* which adds 'Walk Up the Street' and 'Fly into the Mystery' but excludes 'Wake Up, Sleepyheads'.

*Live at the Long Branch and More*; Last Call, 3038212 (France, 1998). The 'more' are previously unreleased versions of 'Modern World', 'Old World', '96 Tears' and 'I'm Straight'.

**ALBUMS** JONATHAN RICHMAN

*Beserkley Chartbusters Vol. 1*; Beserkley, JBZ-0044 (USA, 1975). A compilation that includes four Richman tracks, 'The New Teller', 'Roadrunner', 'Government Center' and 'It Will Stand'.

*Jonathan Richman and the Modern Lovers*; Beserkley, JBZ-0048 (USA, 1976).

*Rock and Roll with the Modern Lovers*; Beserkley, JBZ-0053 (USA, 1977).

*Modern Lovers Live*; Beserkley, JBZ-0055 (USA, 1978).

*Spitballs*; Beserkley, JBZ-0058 (USA, 1978). A compilation that includes one Richman track, a cover of 'Chapel of Love'.

*Back in Your Life*; Beserkley, JBZ-0060 (USA, 1979).

*The Jonathan Richman Songbook*; Beserkley, BSERK 19 (UK, 1980). A withdrawn compilation of previously available material, UK-only release.

*Jonathan Sings!*; Sire, 1-23939 (USA, 1983).

*Rockin' and Romance*; Rough Trade, ROUGH 72 (UK, 1985).

*It's Time for Jonathan Richman and the Modern Lovers*; Rough Trade, ROUGH 92 (UK, 1986).

*The Best of Jonathan Richman and the Modern Lovers*; Rhino, RNCD 75889 (USA, 1986). A CD-only compilation subtitled *The Beserkley Years*, containing material from *The Modern Lovers* plus a long version of 'DodgeVeg-O-Matic', with photographs and a booklet.

*Modern Lovers '88*; Rounder, ROUN 9014 (USA, 1987).

*Jonathan Richman*; Rounder, ROUN 9021 (USA, 1989).

*Gumby*; Buena Vista, 6402 N (USA, 1990). A 'tribute' to the cartoon character that includes one Richman track, 'I Like Gumby'.

*Jonathan Goes Country*; Rounder, ROUN 9024 (USA, 1990).

*Having a Party with Jonathan Richman*; Rounder, ROUN 9026 (USA, 1991).

*I, Jonathan*; Rounder, ROUN 9036 (USA, 1992).

*Jonathan Sings!*; Sire, 9 45284-2 (USA, 1993) A re-release with new sleeve notes and an extra track, a UK B-side, 'The Tag Game'.

*¡Jonathan, Te Vas a Emocionar!*; Rounder, ROUN 9040 (USA, 1994).

*You Must Ask the Heart*, Rounder, ROUN 9047 (USA, 1995).

*Surrender to Jonathan*; Vapor, 9362-46296-2 (USA, 1996).

*Think About Mustapha*; APC, APC 002 (France, 1997). A compilation of versions of the Egyptian folk song 'Mustapha' that includes one by Richman.

*Live From 6A: Conan O'Brien*; Mercury, 314 536 324-2 (USA, 1997). A compilation of live songs from the *Conan O'Brien Show* that includes one Richman track, 'Let Her Go into the Darkness'.

*The Inner Flame*; Atlantic, 83008-2 (USA, 1997). A compilation of material written by Rainer Ptácek that includes one Richman performance, 'Broken Promises'.

*The Unreleasable Tapes*; APC, APC 007 (France, 1997). A compilation that includes one exclusive Richman track, a version of the Aznavour/Roche song 'J'Aime Paris au Mois de Mai'.

*Music From the Motion Picture 'There's Something About Mary'*; Capitol, CDP 7243 49573727 (USA, 1998).

*Roadrunner*; Castle Select, SELCD 521 (UK, 1998). A compilation featuring rare Beserkley material, some never before released on album.

*I'm So Confused*; Vapor, 47086 (USA, 1998).

Jonathan also appears on: 'The Flame Had a Poodle' from Asa Brebner's *Prayers of a Snowball in Hell*, Ocean Music, OM 2008 (USA, 1996); on 'Ensenada', from Ernie Brooks's album *Falling, They Get You*, New Rose,

422501-WM329 (France, 1994), CD only; and on 'Paris in April' by April
March, Sympathy for the Record Industry, SFTRI 456 (USA, 1996).

## SINGLES

'Roadrunner'/'Friday on My Mind'; Beserkley, B-4701 (USA, 1974), with a
    B-side by Earthquake.

'Roadrunner (Once)'/'Roadrunner (Twice)'; Beserkley, BZZ 1 (UK 1976).
    The A-side is the version on *Beserkley Chartbusters* and the B-side is
    from *The Modern Lovers*, the only appearance by the original band on a
    single.

'New England'/'Here Come the Martian Martians'; Beserkley, B-5743
    (USA, 1976).

'Egyptian Reggae'/'Roller Coaster by the Sea'; Beserkley, BZZ 2 (UK,
    1977).

'Morning of Our Lives (Live)'/'Roadrunner Thrice (Live)'; Beserkley,
    BZZ 7 (UK, 1977).

'New England (Live)'/'Astral Plane (Live)'; Beserkley, BZZ 14 (UK, 1977).

'Abdul and Cleopatra'/'Oh Carol'; Beserkley, BZZ 19 (UK, 1978). 'Oh
    Carol' is a version of the Chuck Berry song 'Carol', an out-take from
    *Back in Your Life*.

'Buzz Buzz Buzz'/'Hospital (Live)'; Beserkley, BZZ 25 (UK, 1978).

'I'm Sticking With You'/'Of Yesterday'; Varulven, 805-111 (USA, 1980).
    Jonathan appears on the A-side only, singing a duet with Moe Tucker.

'That Summer Feeling'/'This Kind of Music'/'The Tag Game'; Rough
    Trade, RTT 152 (UK, 1984). 'The Tag Game' previously unreleased
    and only appears on this twelve-inch version.

'I'm Just Beginning to Live'/'Circle I'/'Shirin and Fahrad'; Rough Trade,
    RTT 154 (UK, 1985). The twelve-inch single, 'Circle I', is a different
    version from the one that would later appear on *Modern Lovers '88*;
    'Shirin and Fahrad' is different from the one on 1986's *It's Time for
    Jonathan Richman and the Modern Lovers*.

## CASSETTES

*No Alternative*; Arista, 07822 18737 4 (UK, 1993). An AIDS awareness
    compilation from the Red Hot Organization with one Richman track, a
    previously unreleased live version of 'Hot Nights'. On cassette only.

# OTHER SOURCES

**FURTHER READING**

Bockris, Victor and Gerard Malanga, *Up-tight: The Story of the Velvet Underground*, London: Omnibus Press, 1996. Includes Jonathan's account of the instruments and amplification used by the Velvet Underground.

Burchill, Julie and Tony Parsons, *'The Boy Looked at Johnny'*, London: Pluto Press, 1978. Includes a section on Jonathan in which *The Modern Lovers* is described as 'the most innovative record in the history of rock'.

Cohen, Scott, *Yakety Yak*, New York: Fireside/Simon and Schuster, 1994. Includes a revamped version of Cohen's 1973 article in *Interview* and some good photographs of the original Modern Lovers.

Griffin, Sid, *Gram Parsons: A Music Biography*, Pasadena: Sierra Books, 1985. Includes Kim Fowley talking about the Modern Lovers and features one of their press photographs.

Heylin, Clinton, *From the Velvets to the Voidoids*, Harmondsworth: Penguin, 1993. Includes a chapter on the original Modern Lovers.

Kaufman, Phil with Colin White, *Road Mangler Deluxe*, Glendale: White Boucke Publishing, 1993. An account of Kaufman's years as a road manager, including reminiscences of his time with the original Modern Lovers and a photograph of the band playing at Gram Parsons's wake, Kaufman's Koffin Kaper Konsert.

Marcus, Greil, *Lipstick Traces*, London: Secker and Warburg, 1989. Includes a piece on 'Roadrunner'.

Schinder, Scott and the Editors of Rolling Stone Press, *Rolling Stone's Alt-Rock-a-Rama*, New York: Delta Trade Paperbacks, 1996. Includes a number of references to Jonathan.

Vowell, Sarah, *Radio On: A Listener's Diary*, New York: St Martin's Press, 1996. Includes Vowell's reflections on her love of Jonathan's music and her reactions to hearing him on the radio.

Wallechinsky, David and Amy Wallace, *The Book of Lists: The 90s Edition*, London: Aurum Press, 1994. Includes a list of Jonathan's favourite singers.

## BACKGROUND MATERIAL

Bangs, Lester, 'Richman? Poor, Man', *New Musical Express*,
   13 August 1977

Birch, Ian, 'In Love with the Modern World', *Melody Maker*,
   19 September 1977

Dadomo, Giovanni, 'A Run on the Wild Side', *Sounds*, 3 July 1976

Dadomo, Giovanni, 'A Sense of Wonder', *Sounds*, 25 June 1977

Flanagan, Bill, 'The Modern Lovers', *Trouser Press*, November 1979

Holdship, Bill, 'Shoot-out at Sesame Street: Jonathan Richman Talks!',
   *Creem*, 1983

Kaplan, Ira, 'Jonathan Richman, Bijou Café, Phil.', *New York Rocker*,
   November 1979

Lethem, Jonathan, 'Jonathan Richman', *Pulse!*, October 1996

Matthews, Jane, 'Rich Man, Poor Man', *Zigzag*, October 1984

Needs, Kris, 'Jonathan', *Zigzag*, November 1977

Persky, Lisa Jane, 'Transactional Analysis at Town Hall', *New York Rocker*,
   December 1976

Radin, Robin, 'Train Ride with Jonathan', *New York Rocker*, June/July 1979

Rambali, Paul, '"Time for Bed!" Said Jonathan', *New Musical Express*,
   13 August 1977

Ruth, Emma, 'Jonathan Richman, Leeds Poly', *New Musical Express*,
   29 June 1978

Savage, Jon, 'Jonathan Richman, Hammersmith Odeon', *New Musical
   Express*, 24 September 1977

Zeller, Craig, 'A Roadrunner for Your Love', *New York Rocker*, October 1977

## USEFUL WEBSITES

Please note that the information given in this section was accurate as of
summer 1999, but these things come and go, so some of the sites may have
ceased to operate and others may have come into being even before this
book goes to press.

### OFFICIAL RECORD COMPANY SITES

http://www.tt.net/twintone/richman.html – Twin/Tone page
http://harp.rounder.com/rounder/catalog/byartist/r/richman_jonathan – Rounder page
http://www.vaporrecords.com/jonathan40.htm – Vapor page

### SITES EXCLUSIVELY ABOUT JONATHAN

http://www.base.com/jonathan/jonathan.html – the Abominable Lesbian Vampire
   Cappuccino Bar in Cyberspace, a great site full of information and links
   and with access to the Jonathan Richman Mailing List

http://www.dirtywater.com/a2z/r/richman/harvard.html – Boston Rock Storybook, the
   first of a succession of fascinating pages on the history of the Modern
   Lovers
http://members.aol.com/boutndrose/jrp – the Jonathan Richman Project, a fine
   fanzine by Tony Jonaitis and Rich Hager
http://users.ids.net/~dmsr/jrlinks.html – Jonathan Richman Links
http://www.hippywig.demon.co.uk – Simes's Jonathan Richman Pages, with plenty
   of useful background material
http://www.downrecs.com/jrich.asp – Download Recordings Music Video Archive,
   featuring full streaming versions of the videos for 'I'm So Confused' and
   'I Was Dancing in the Lesbian Bar', together with a downloadable
   segment of the latter

COMMERCIAL SITES WITH LINKS TO PAGES EXCLUSIVELY ABOUT JONATHAN
http://www.musicblvd.com – Music Boulevard, providing access to a list of CDs
   available from this website and a good selection of links to related
   articles
http://www.rollingstone.com – Rolling Stone Network, providing access to a
   series of informative pages

# INDEX